DYLANNA PRESS

FOX

COLORING BOOK FOR ADULTS

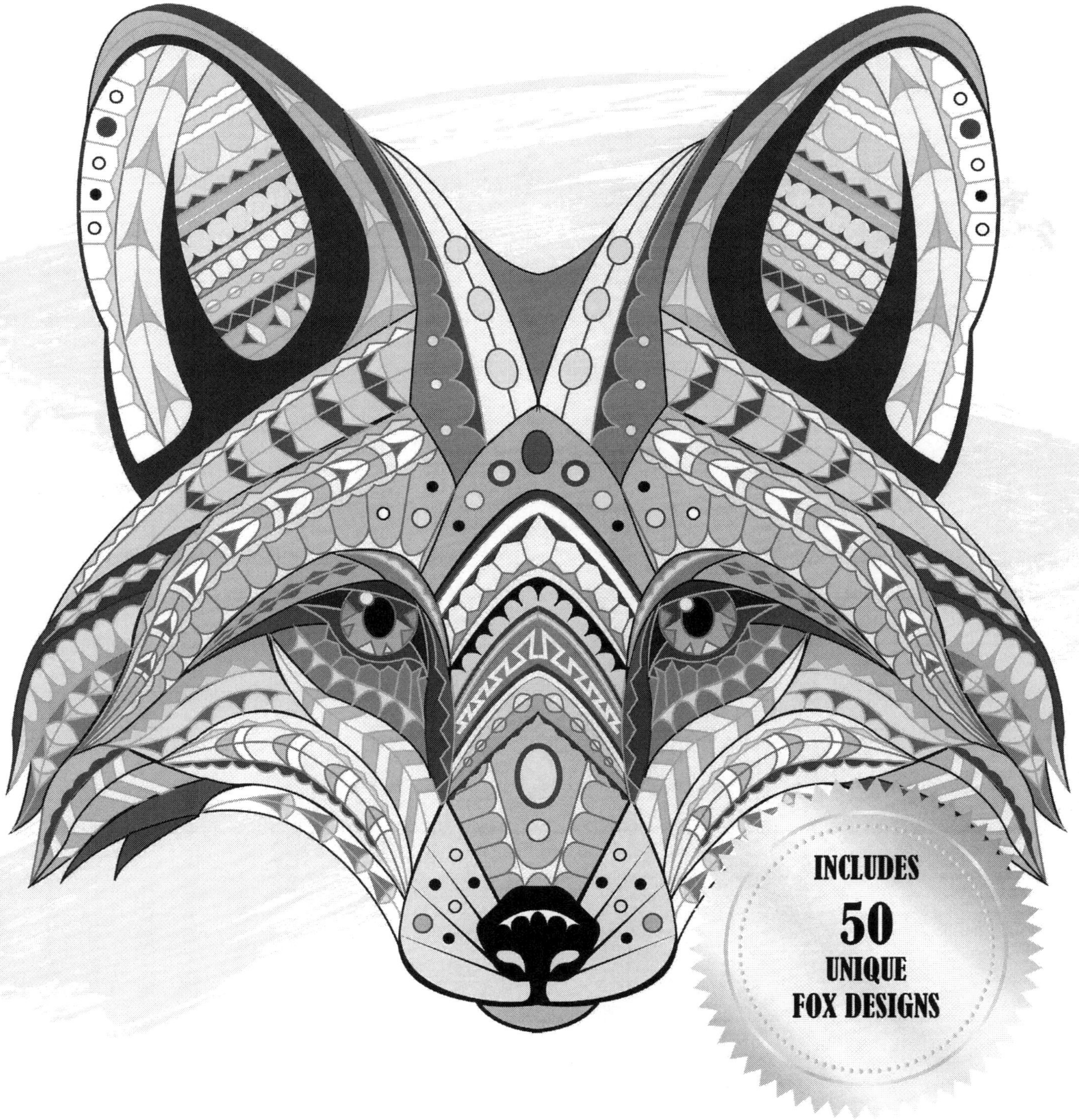

INCLUDES 50 UNIQUE FOX DESIGNS

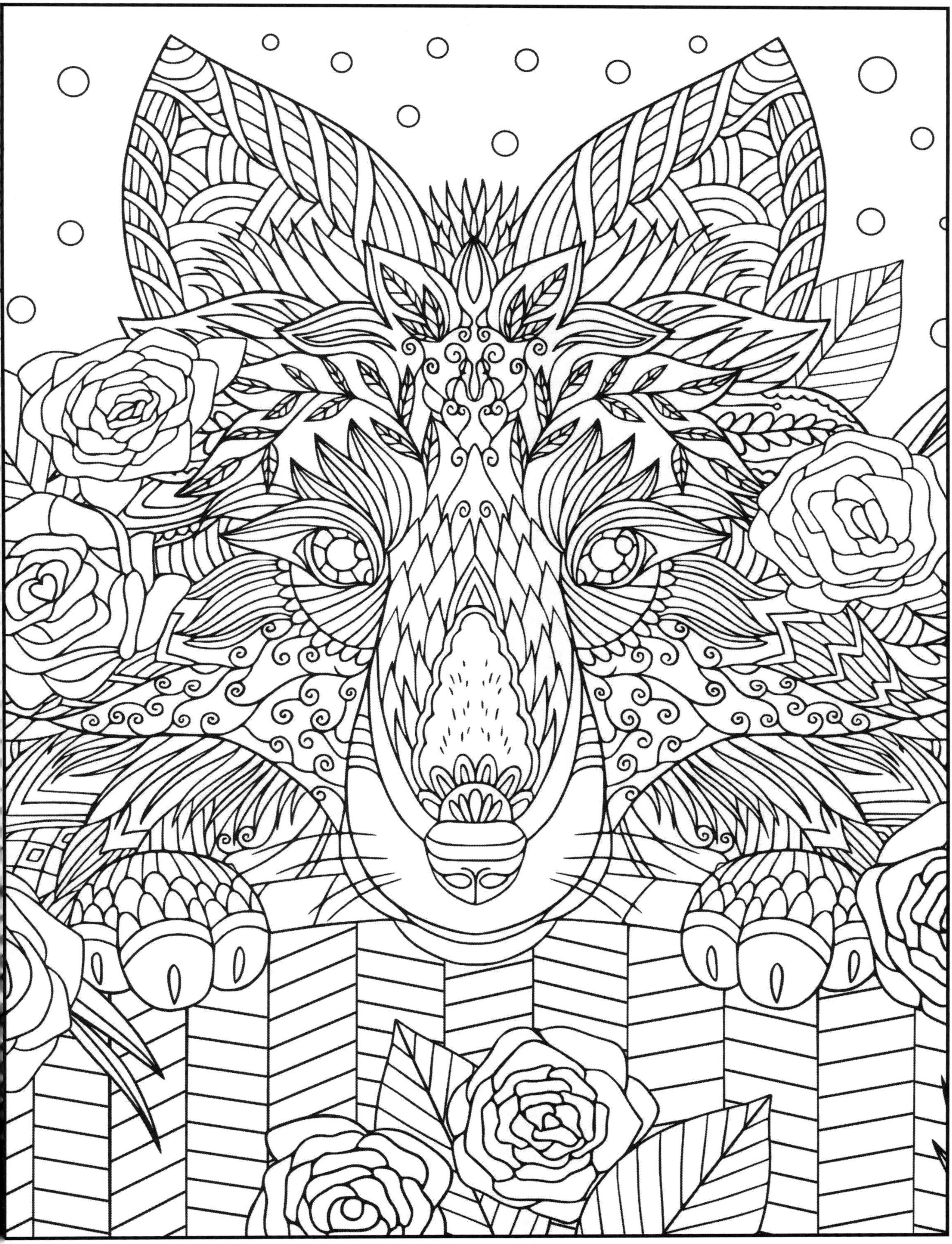

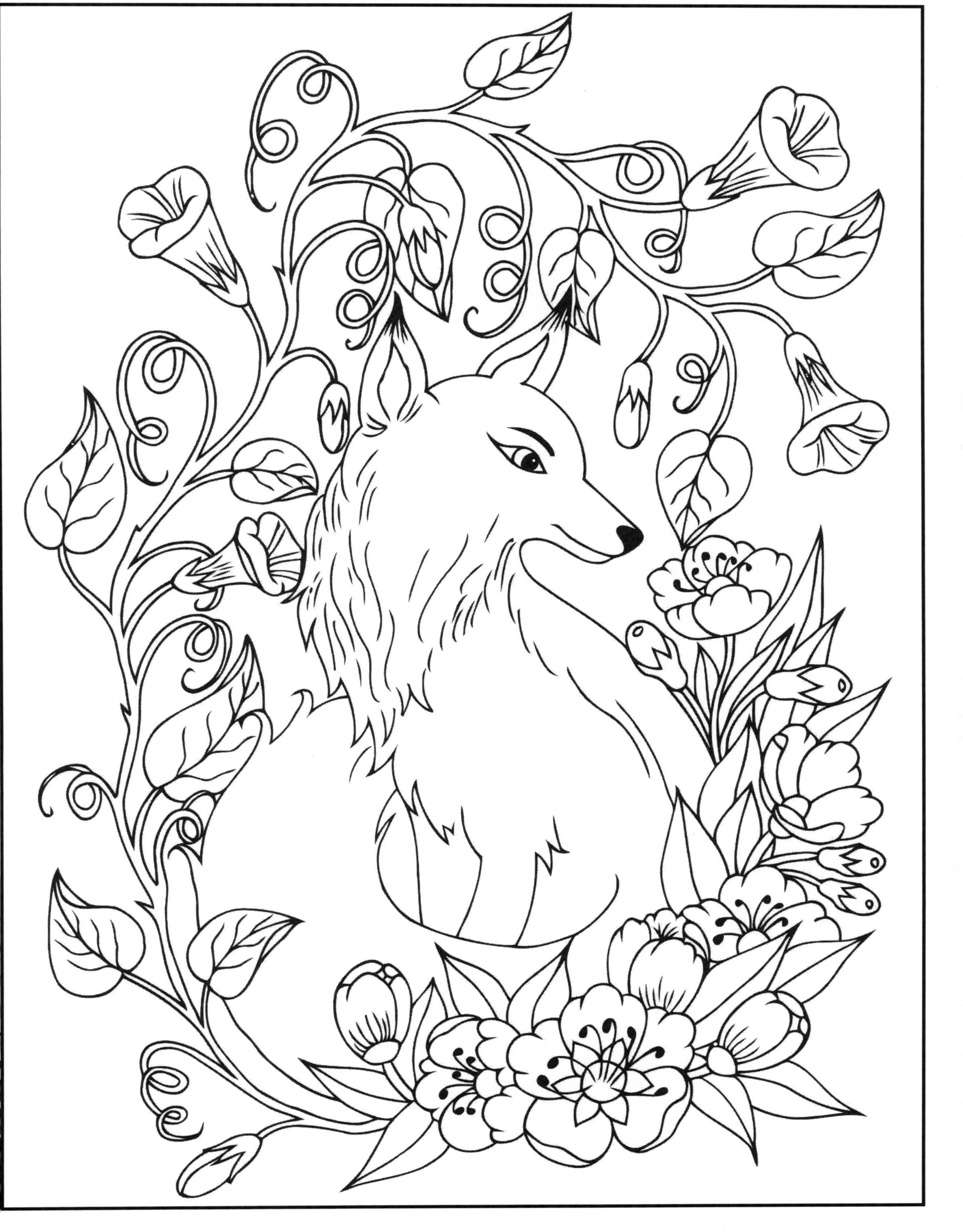

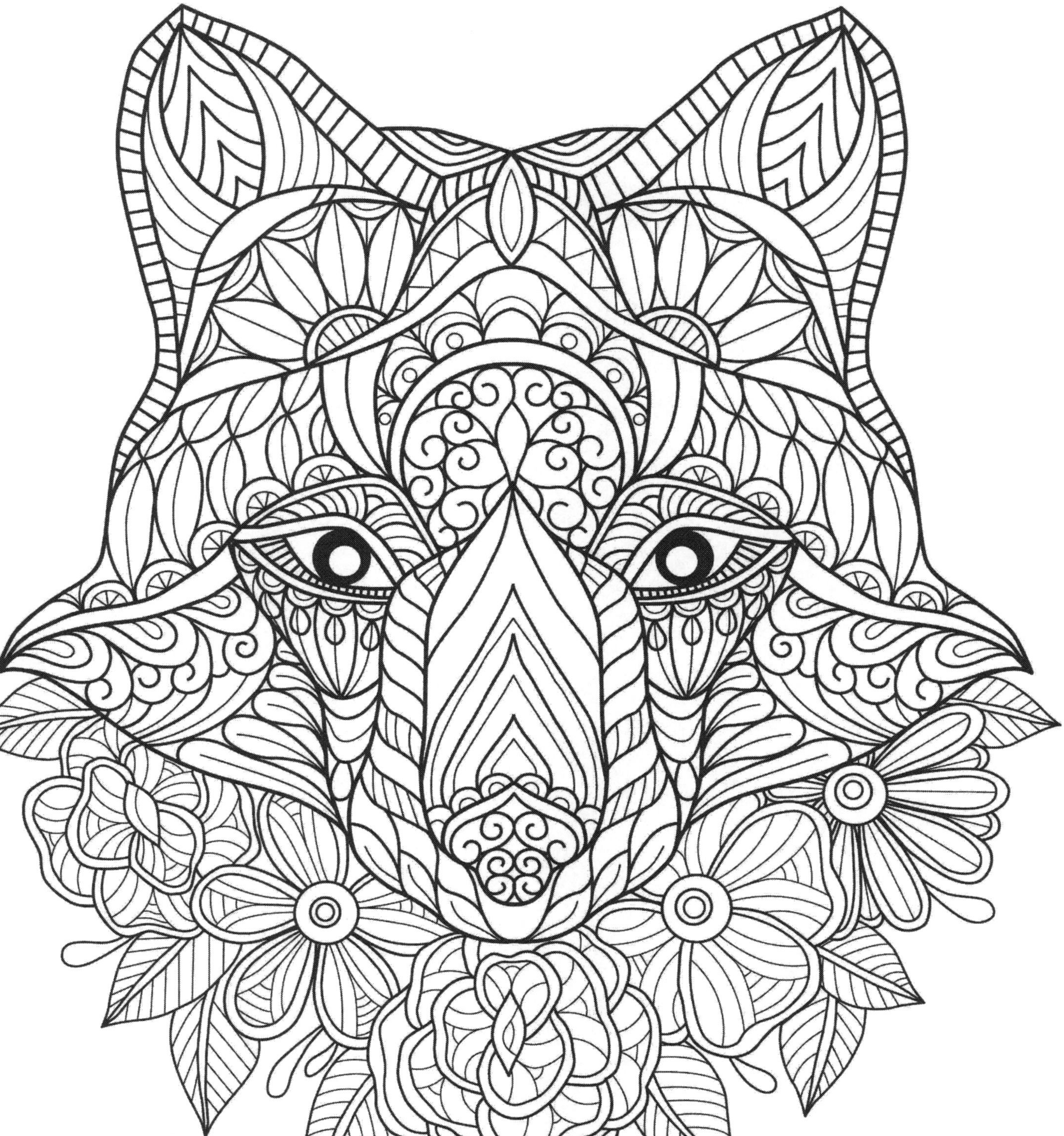

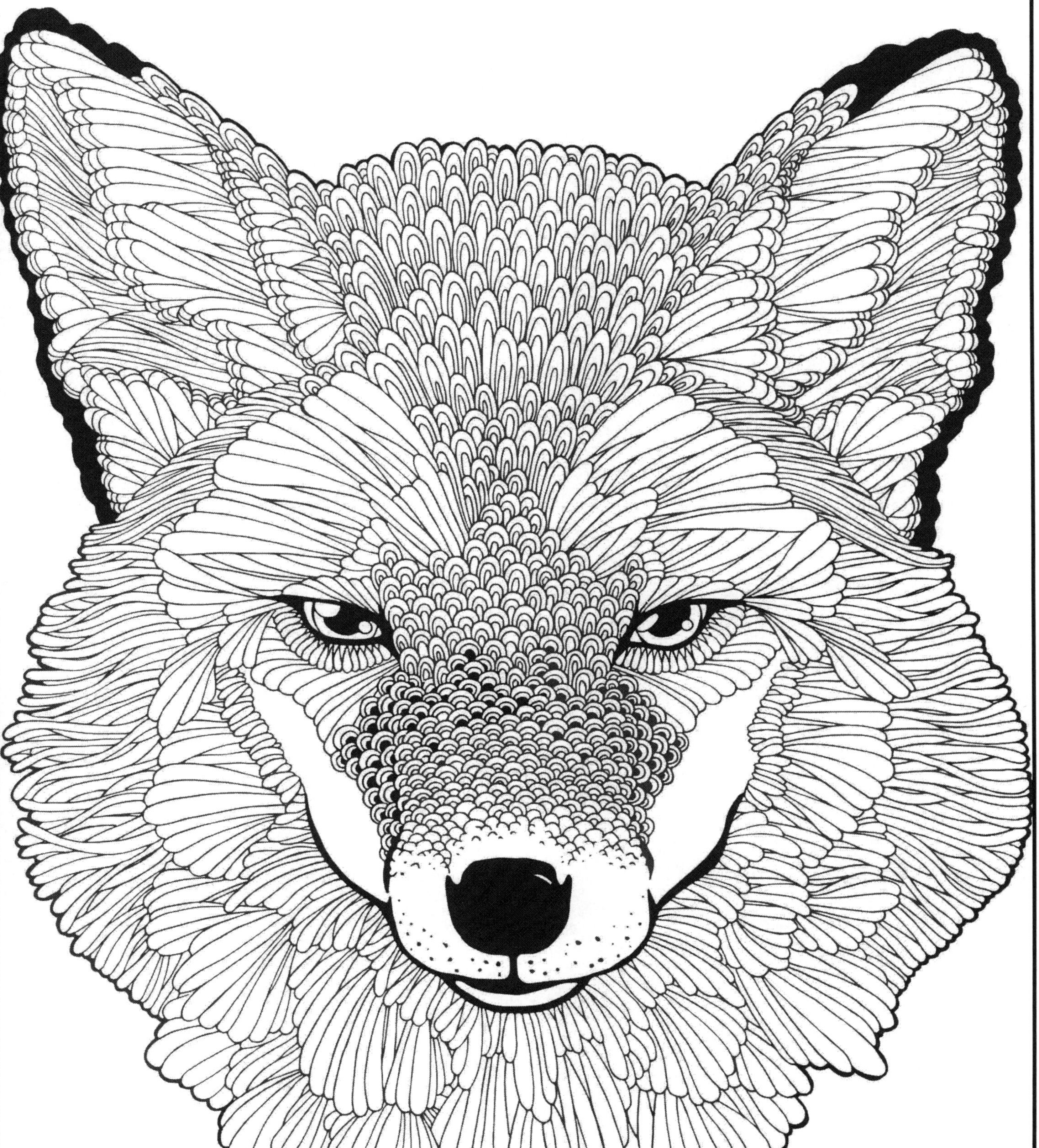

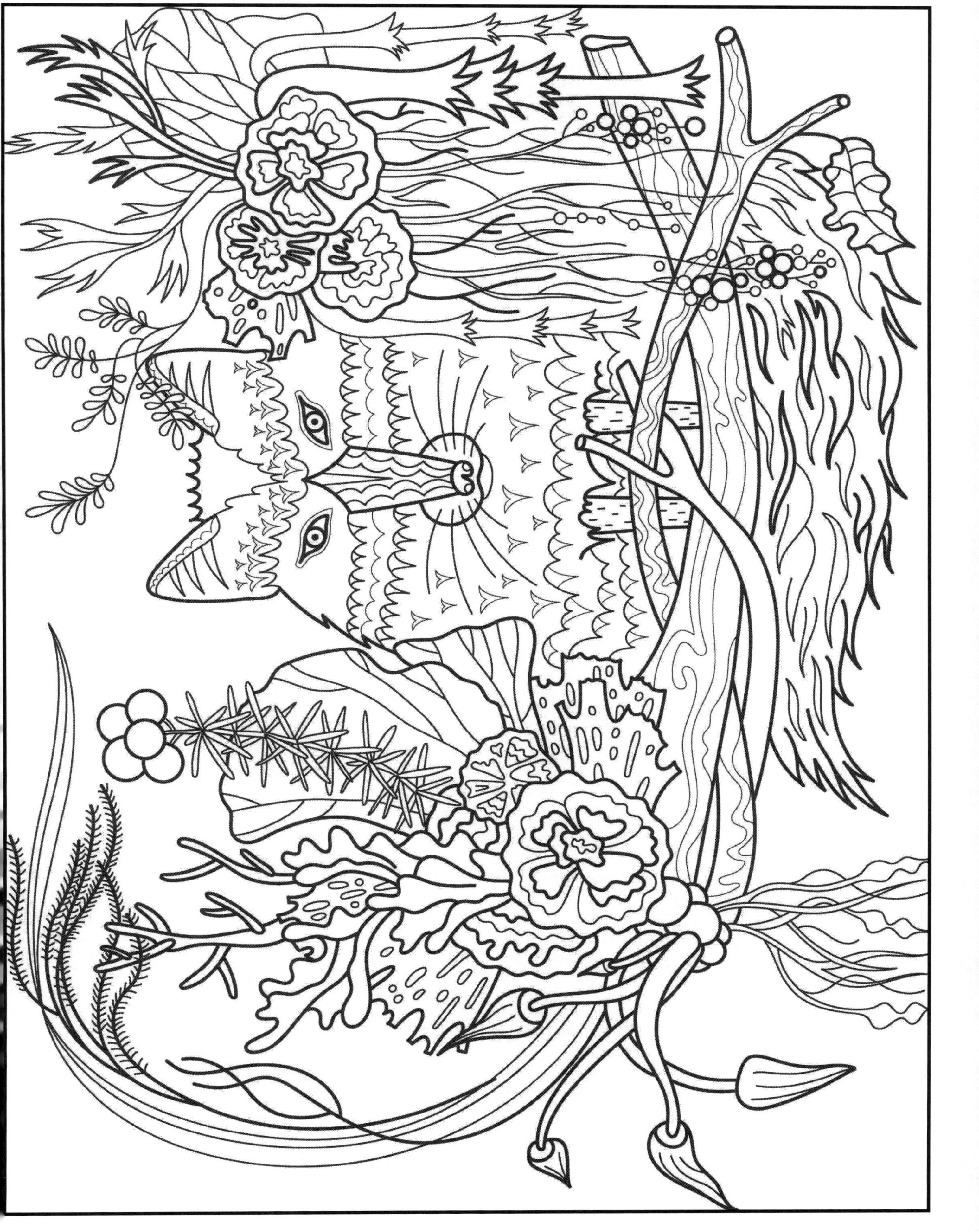

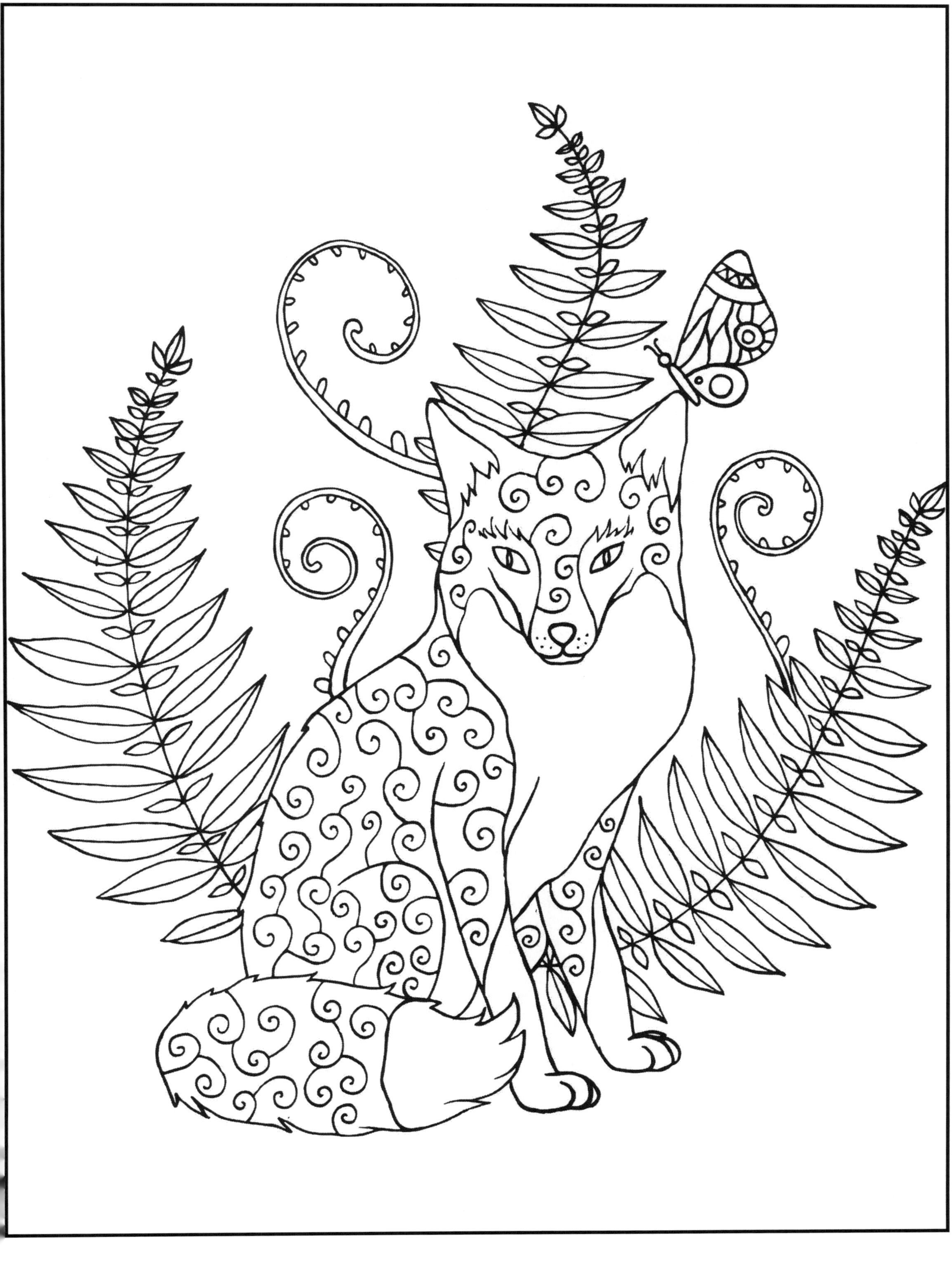

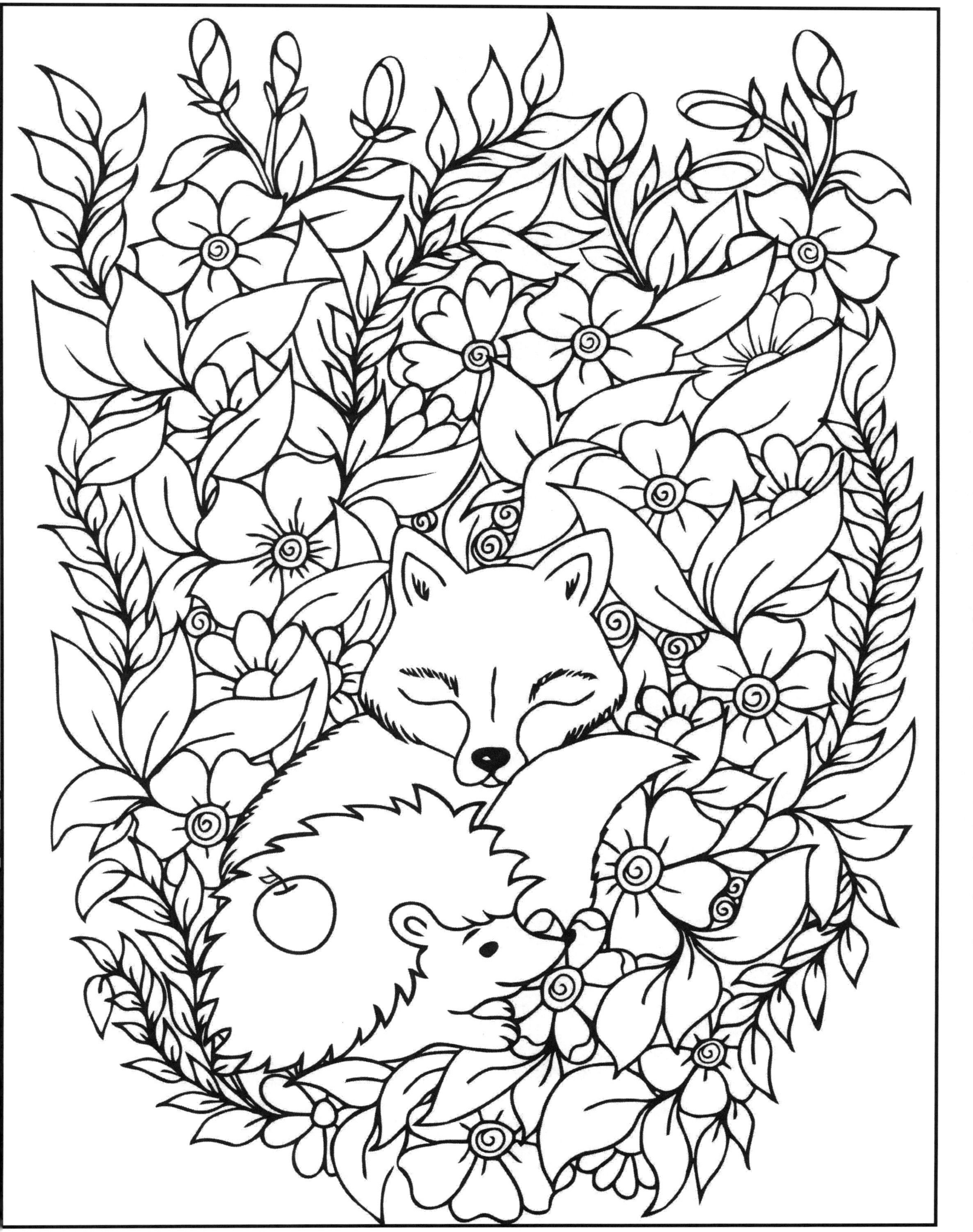

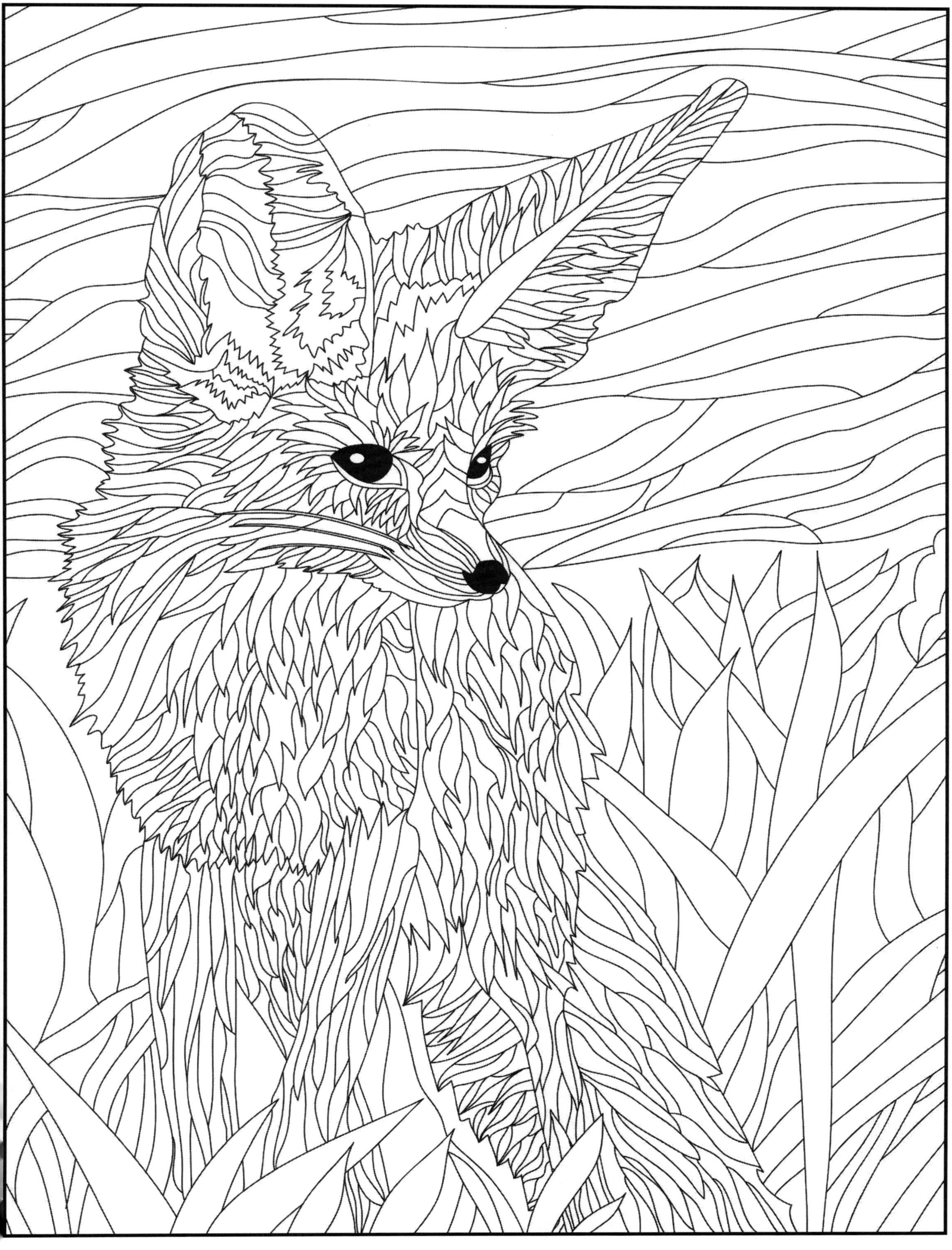

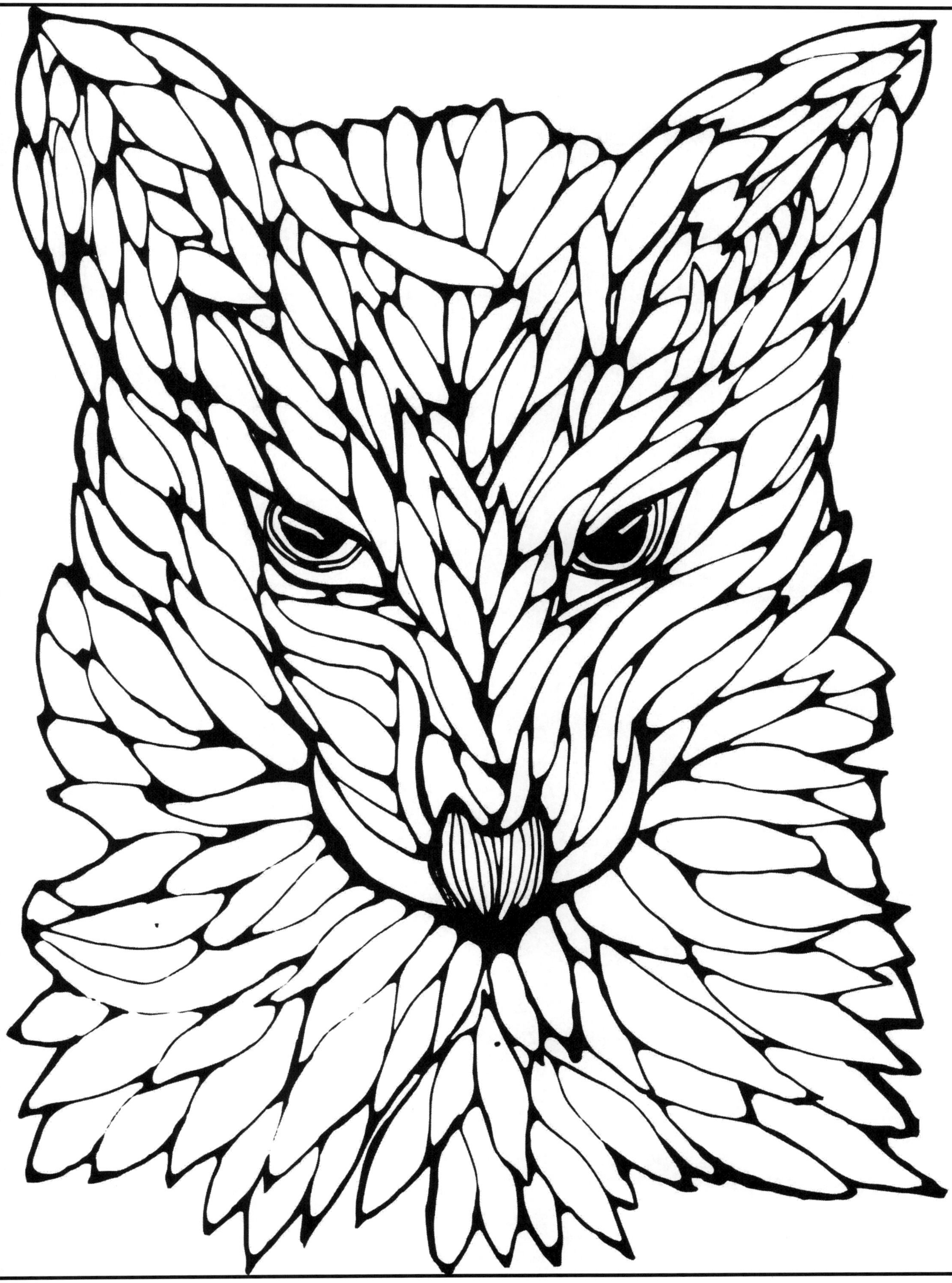

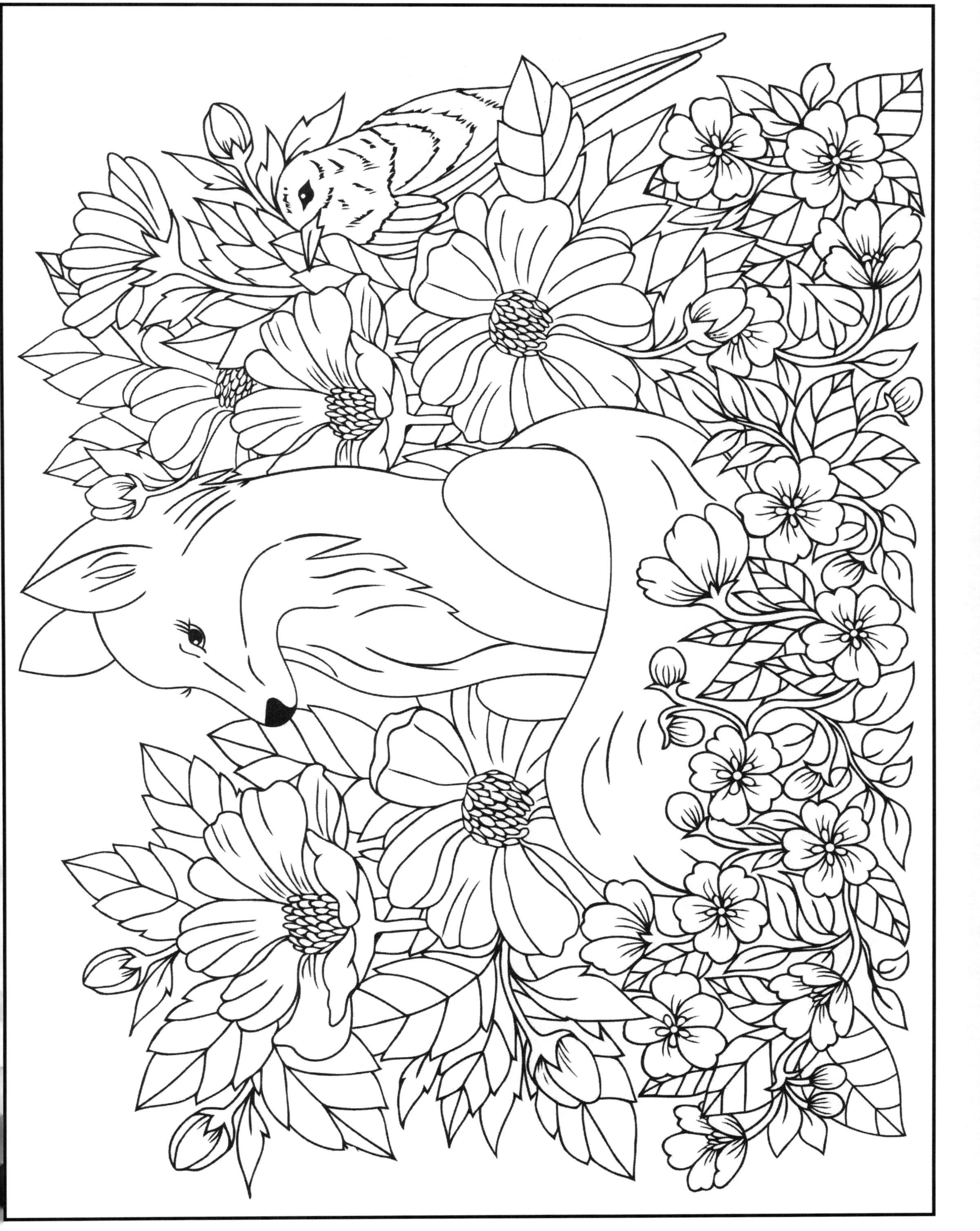

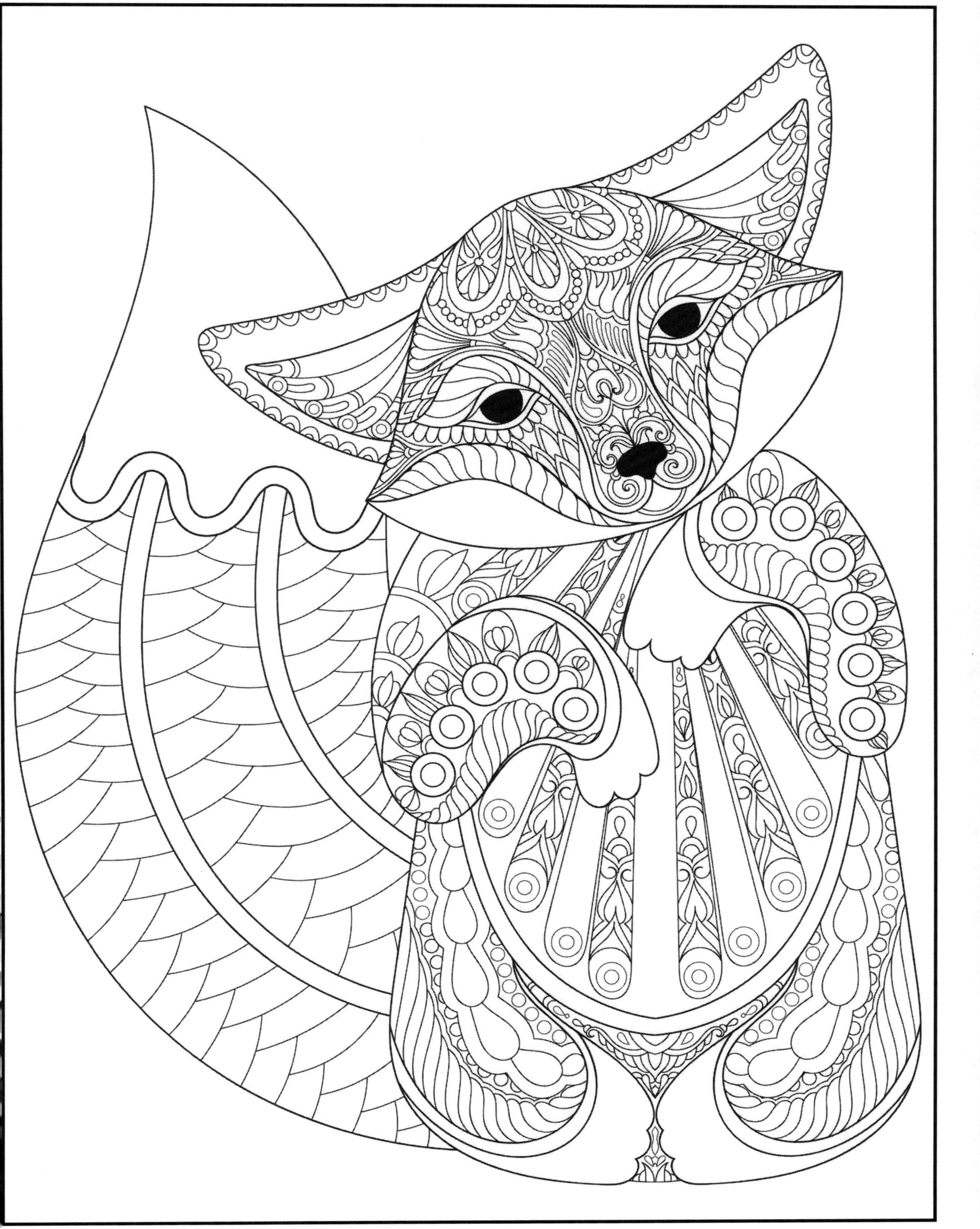

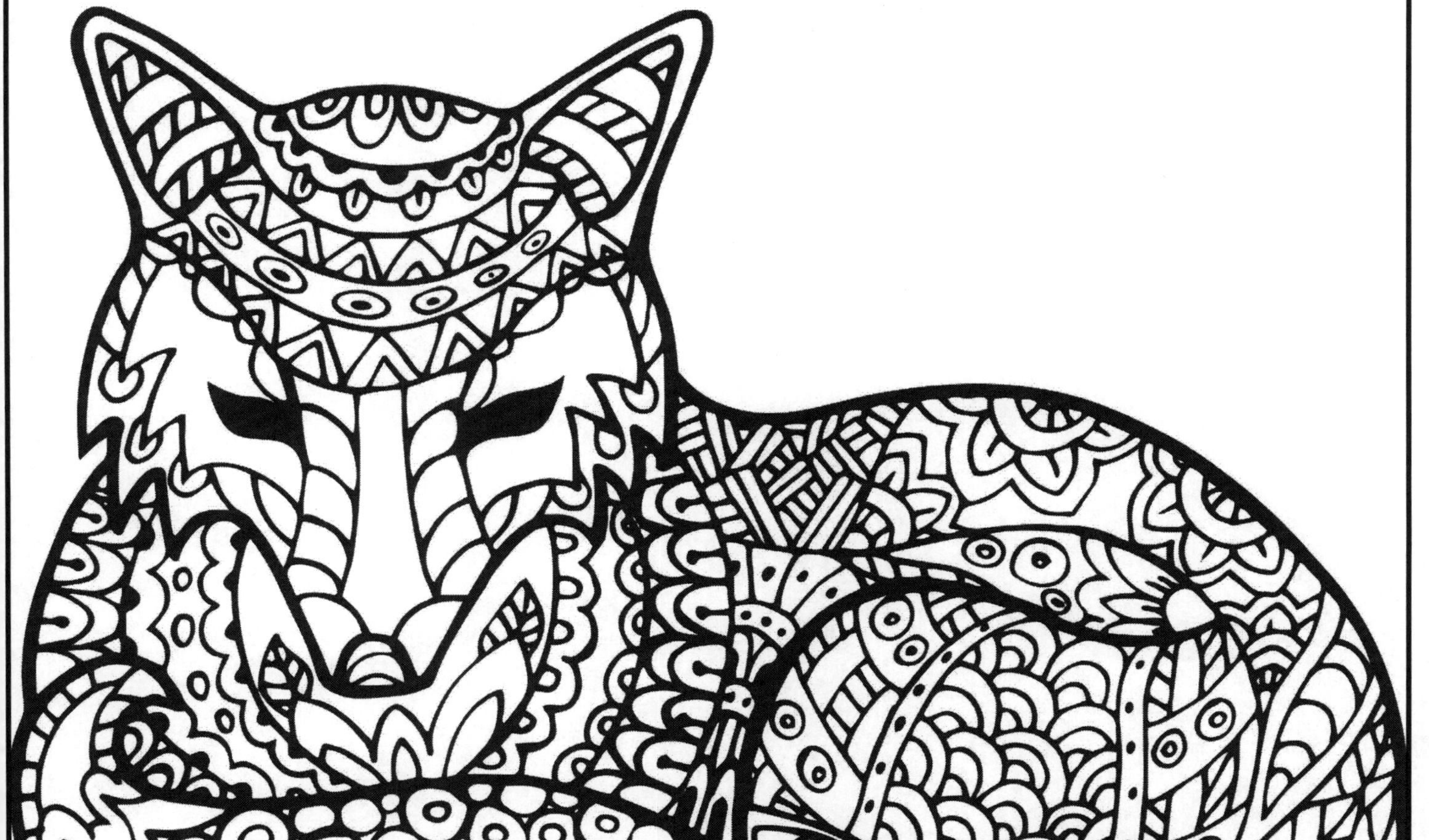

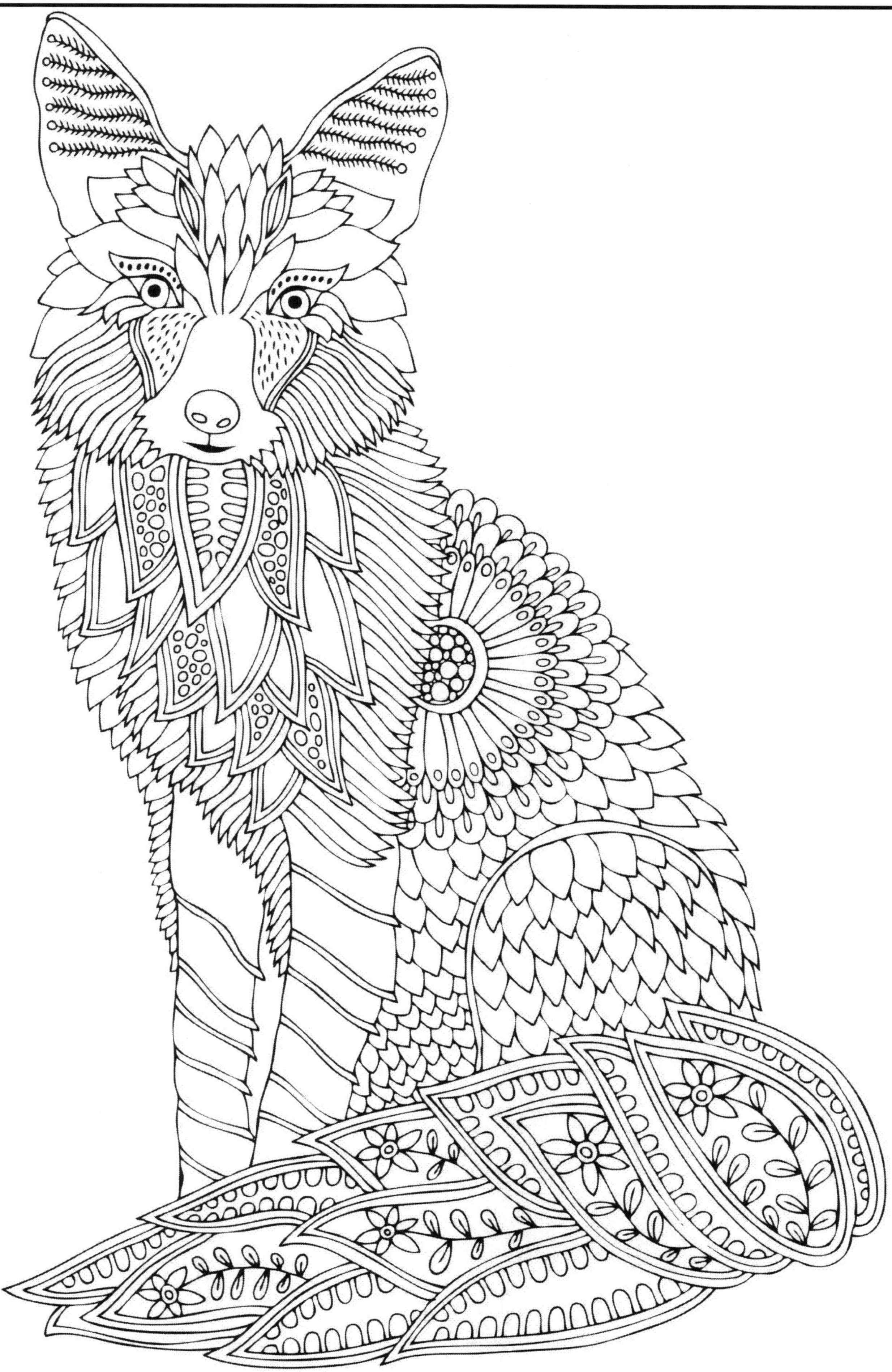

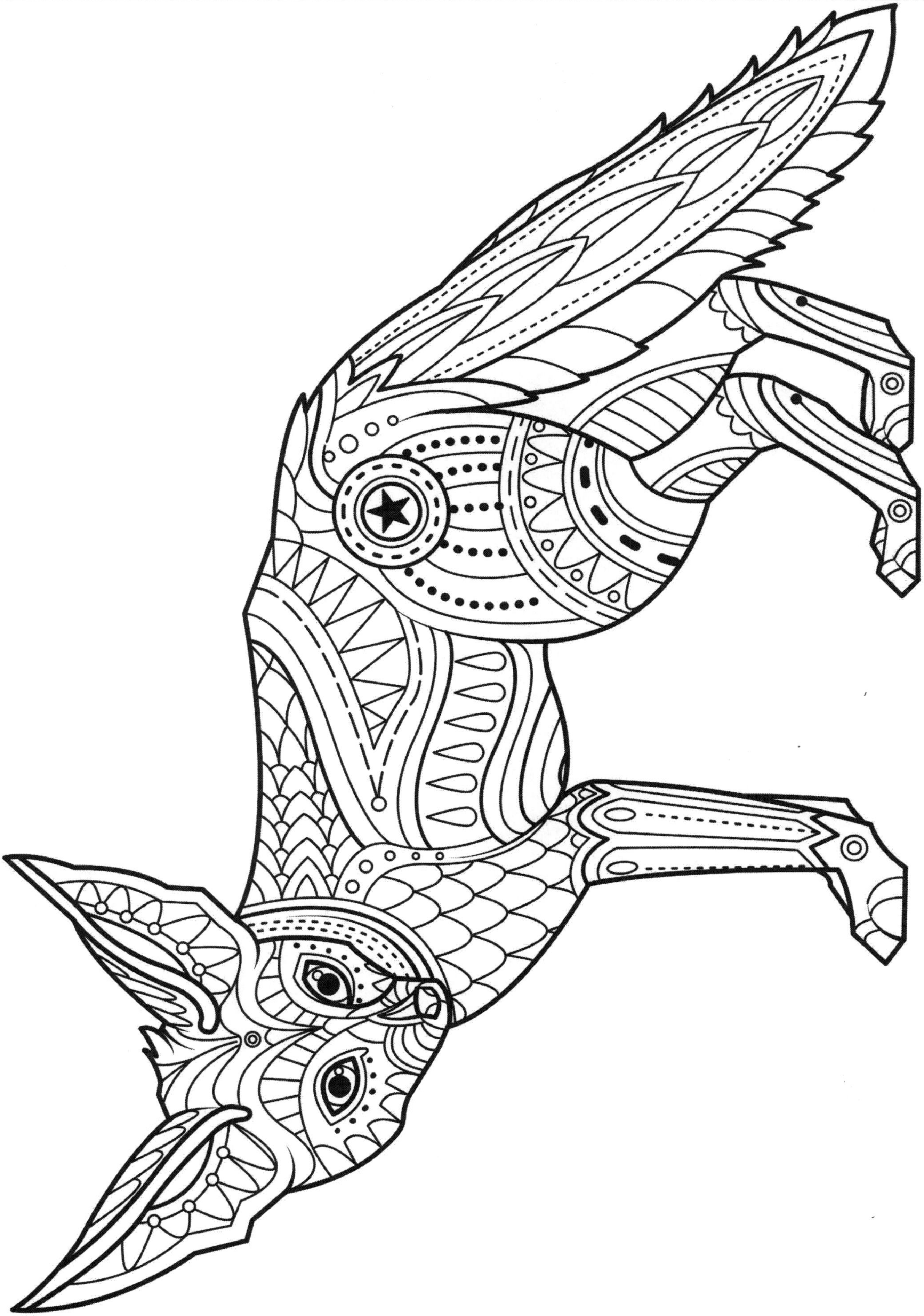

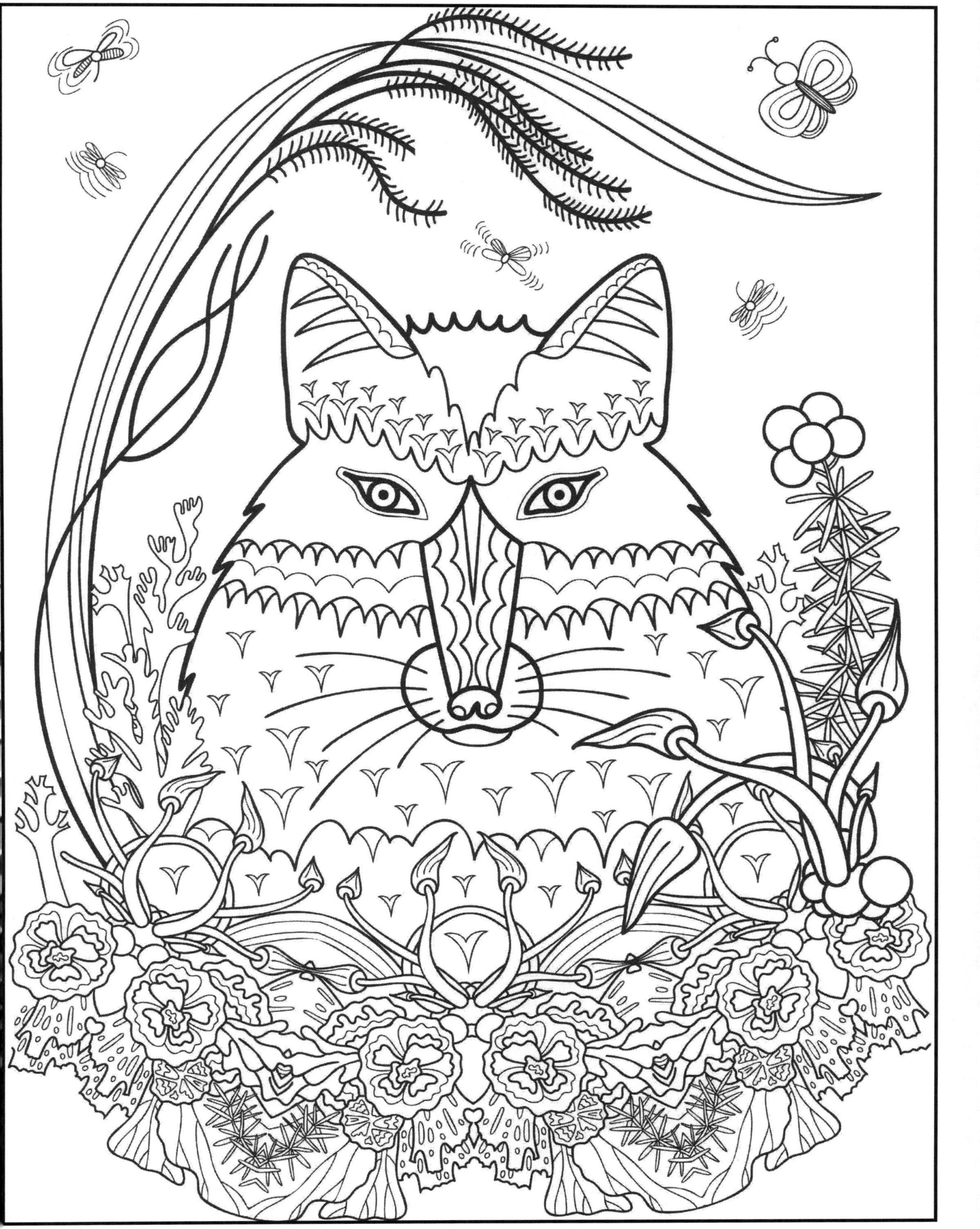

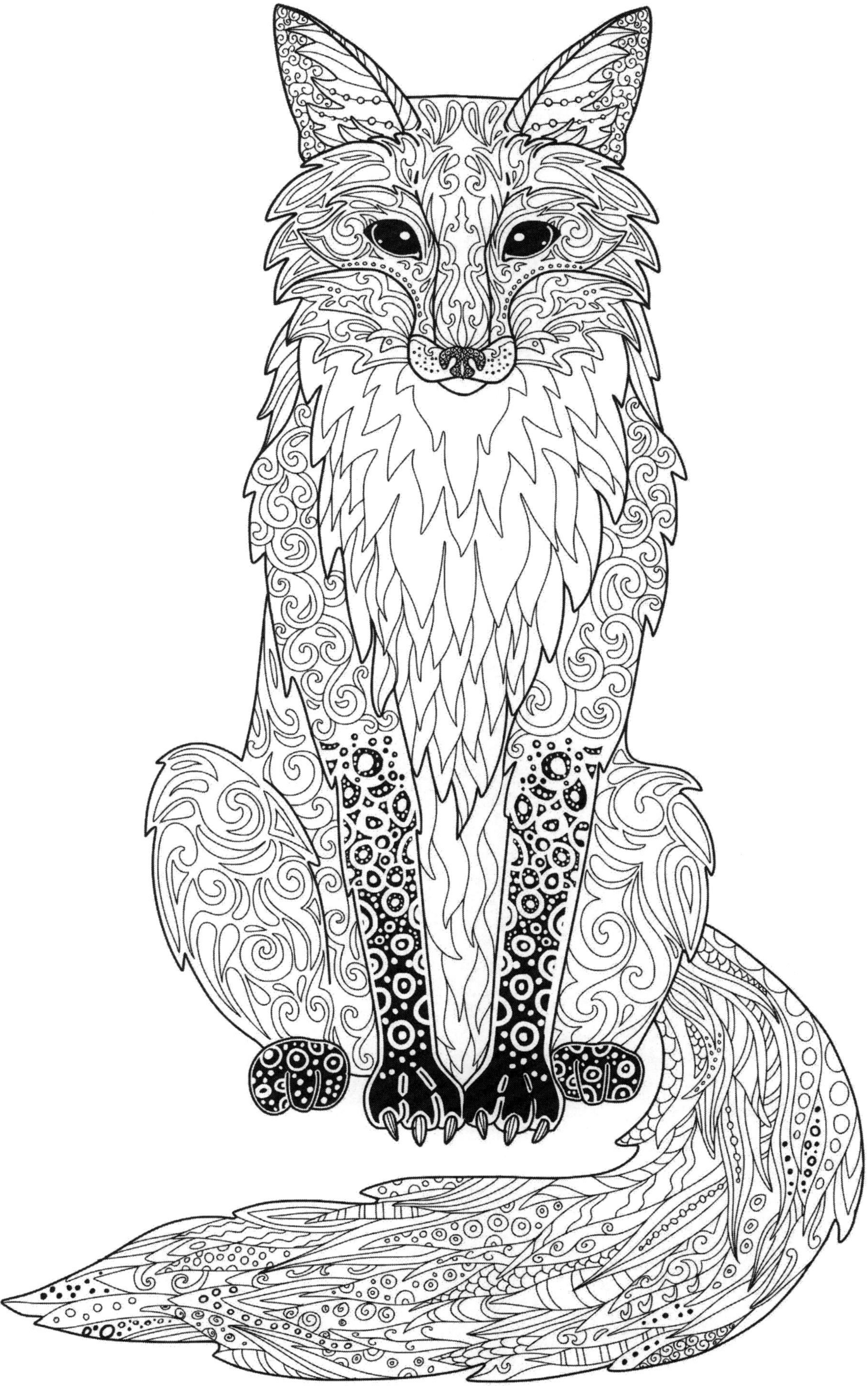

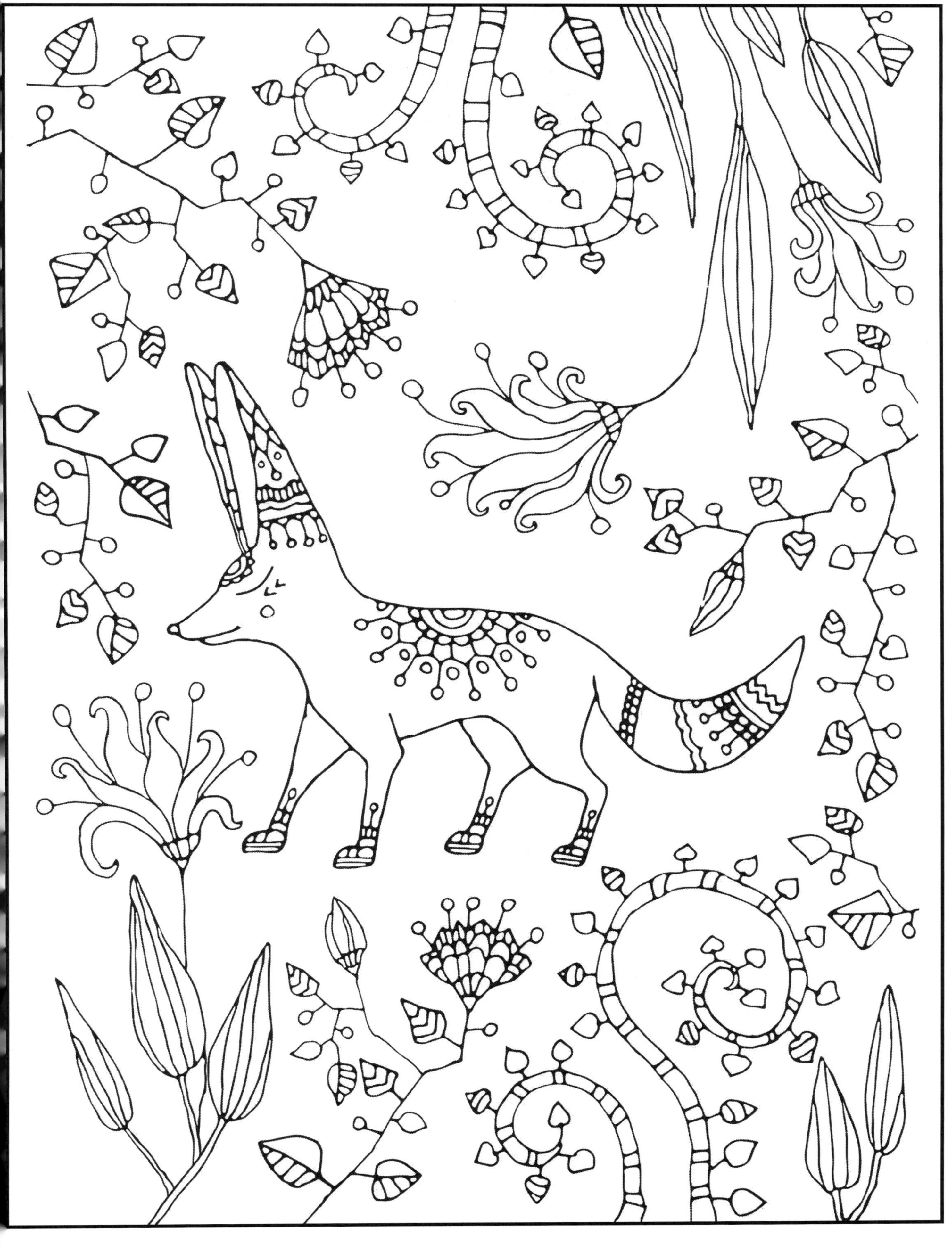

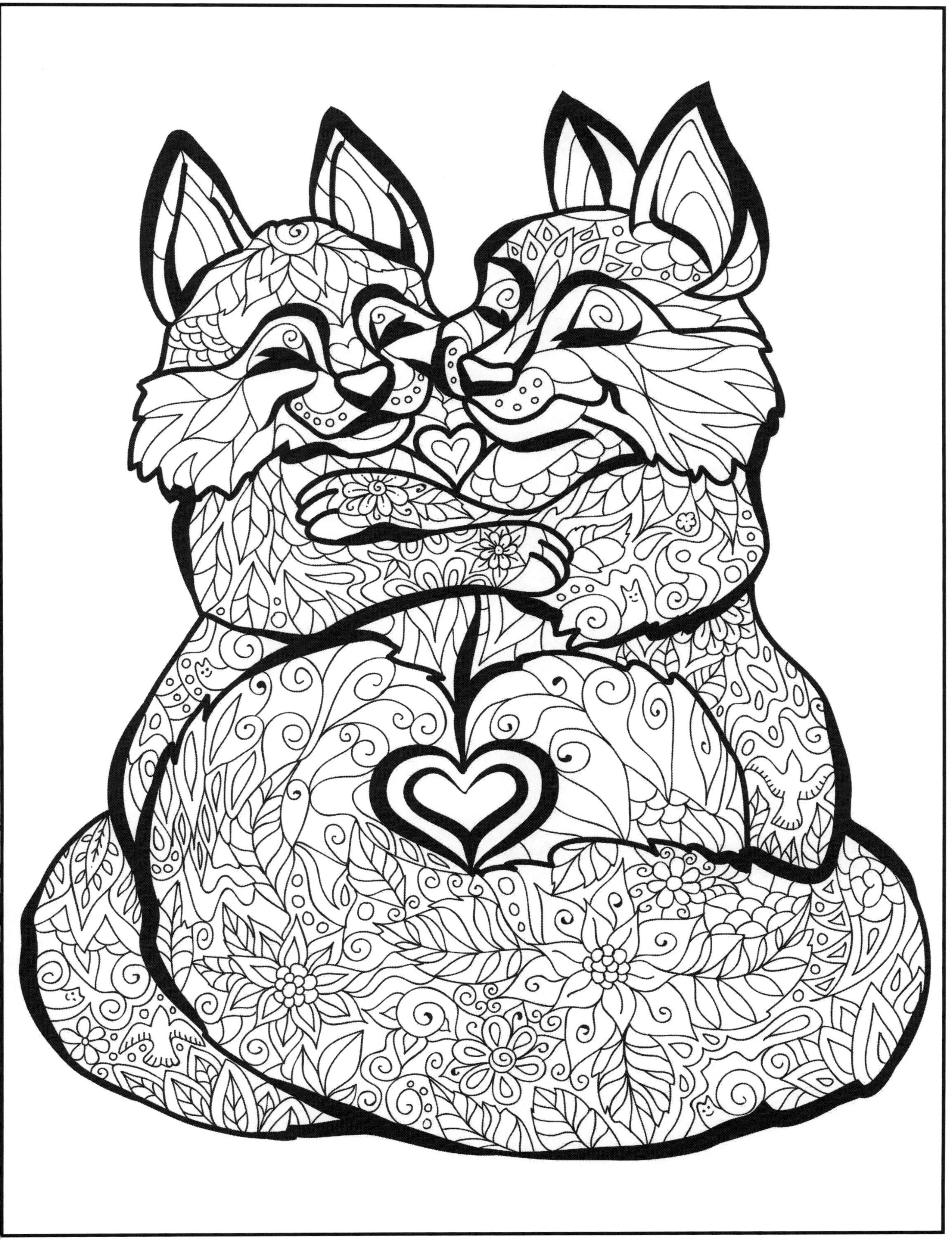

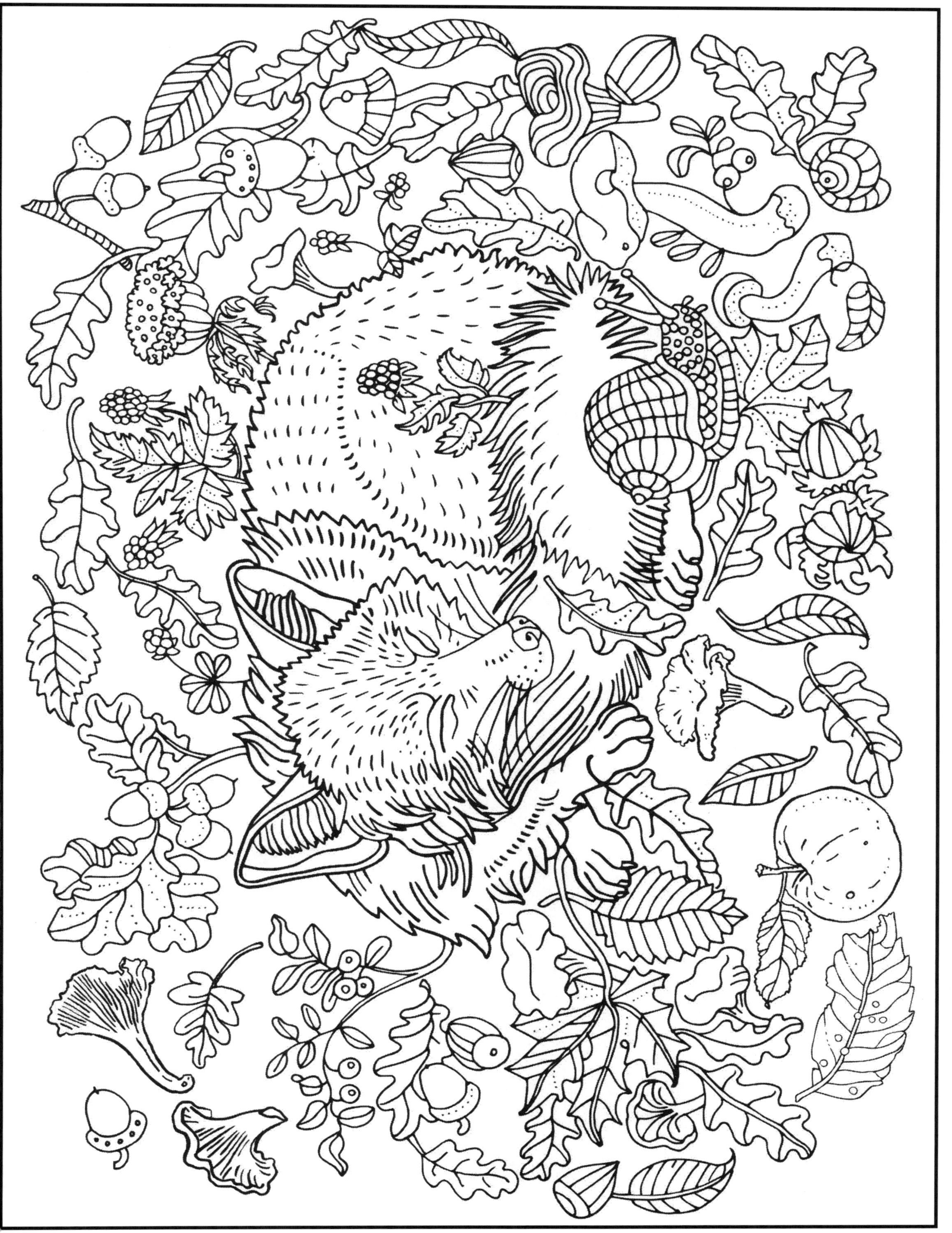

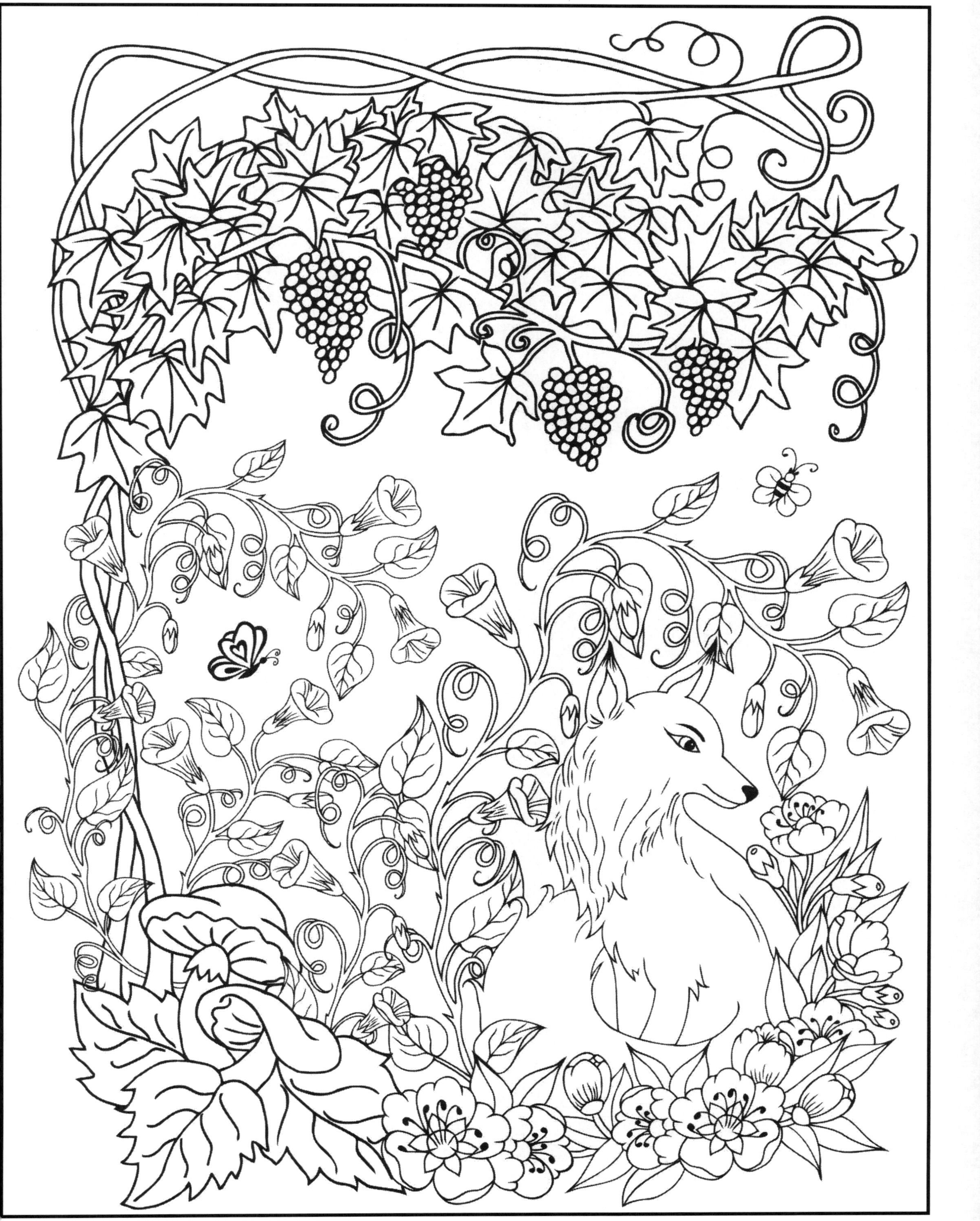

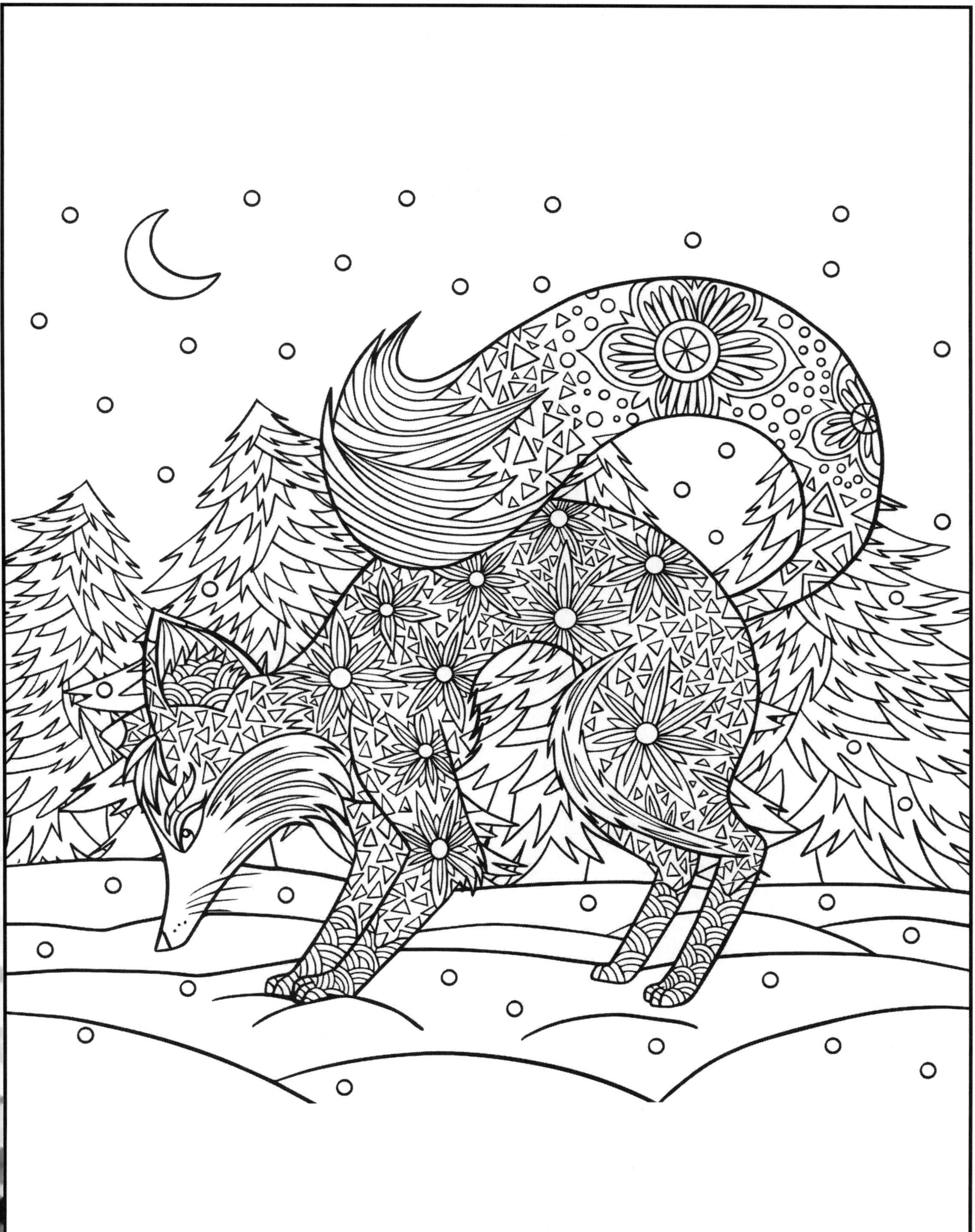

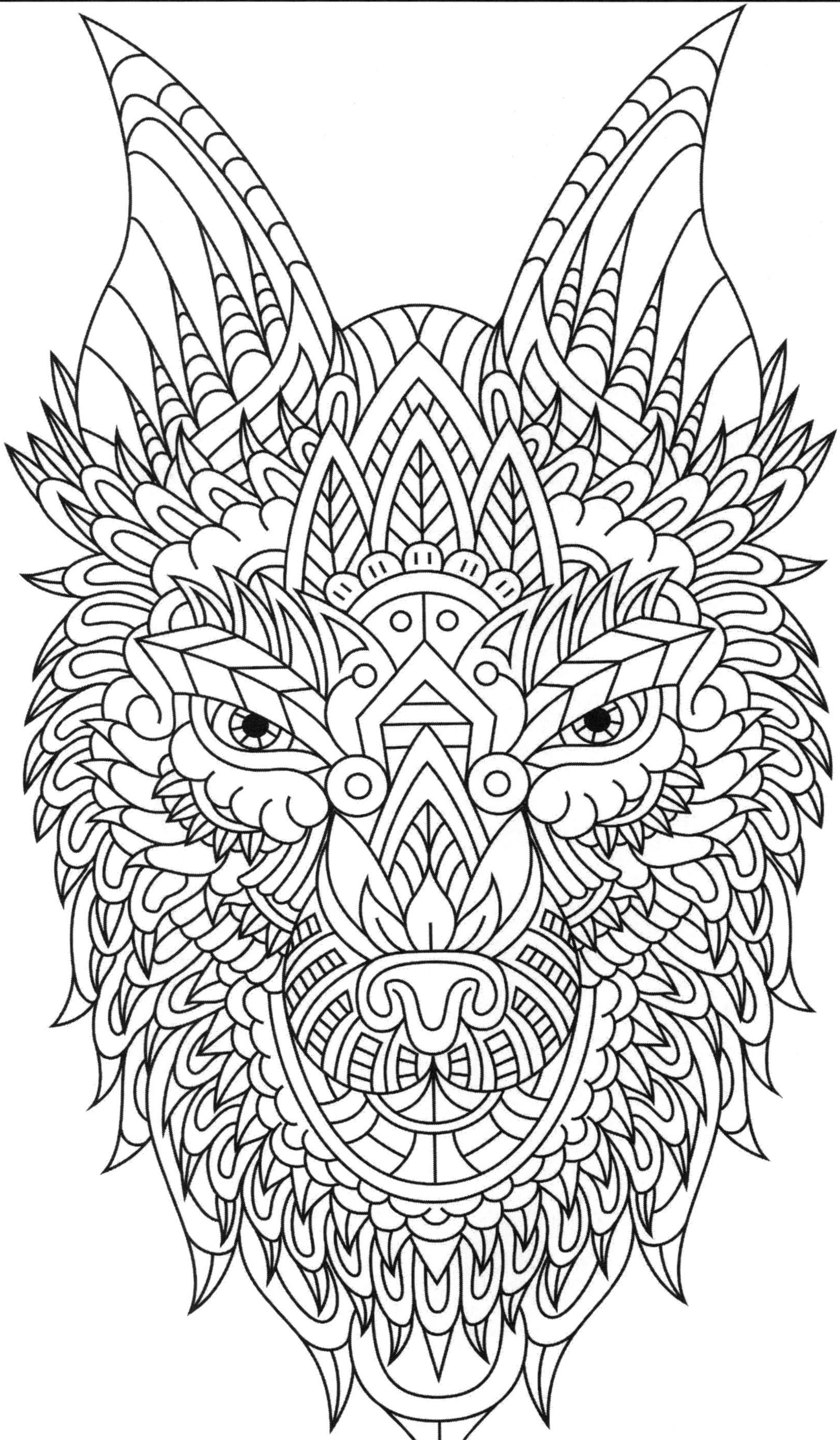

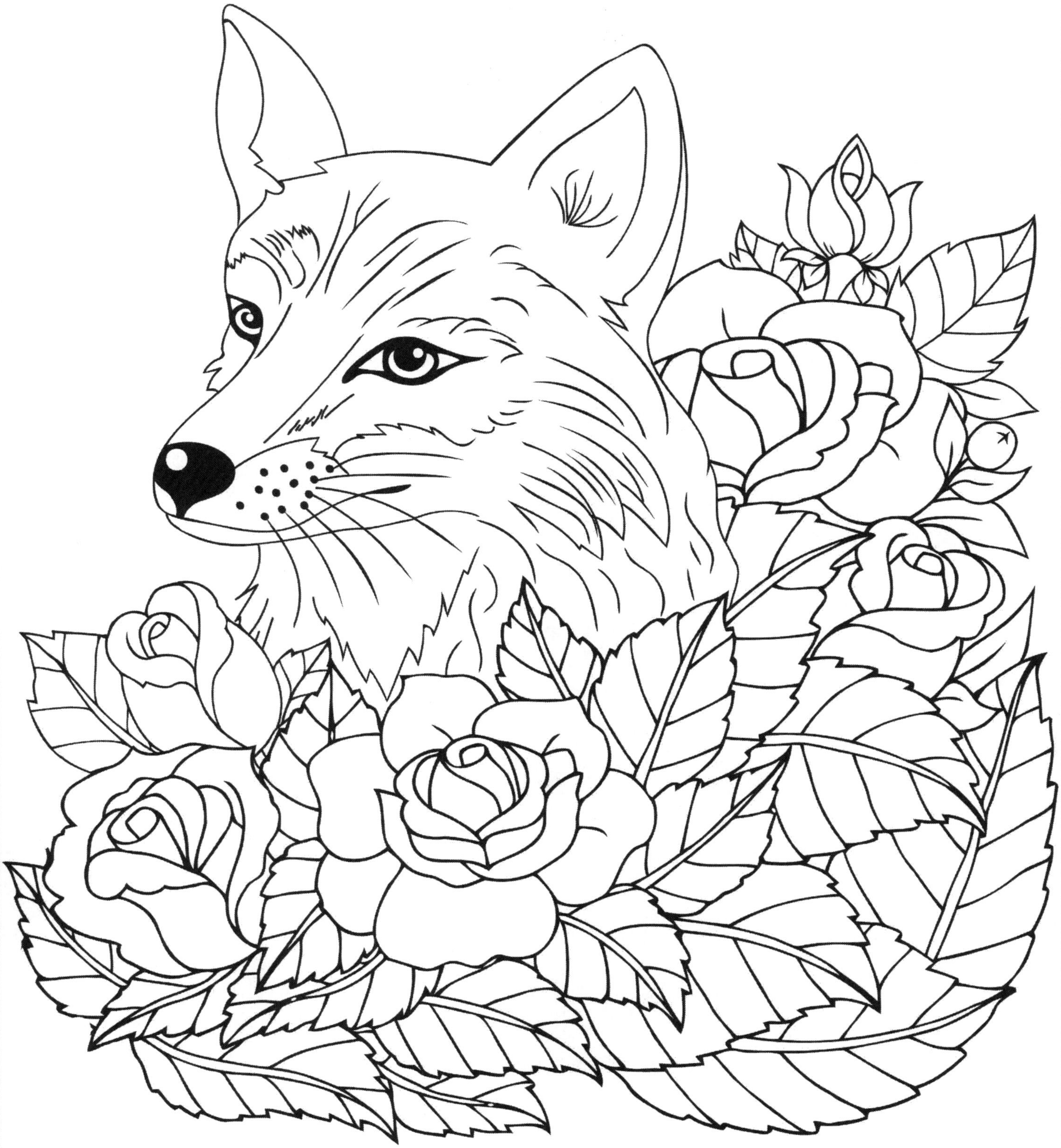

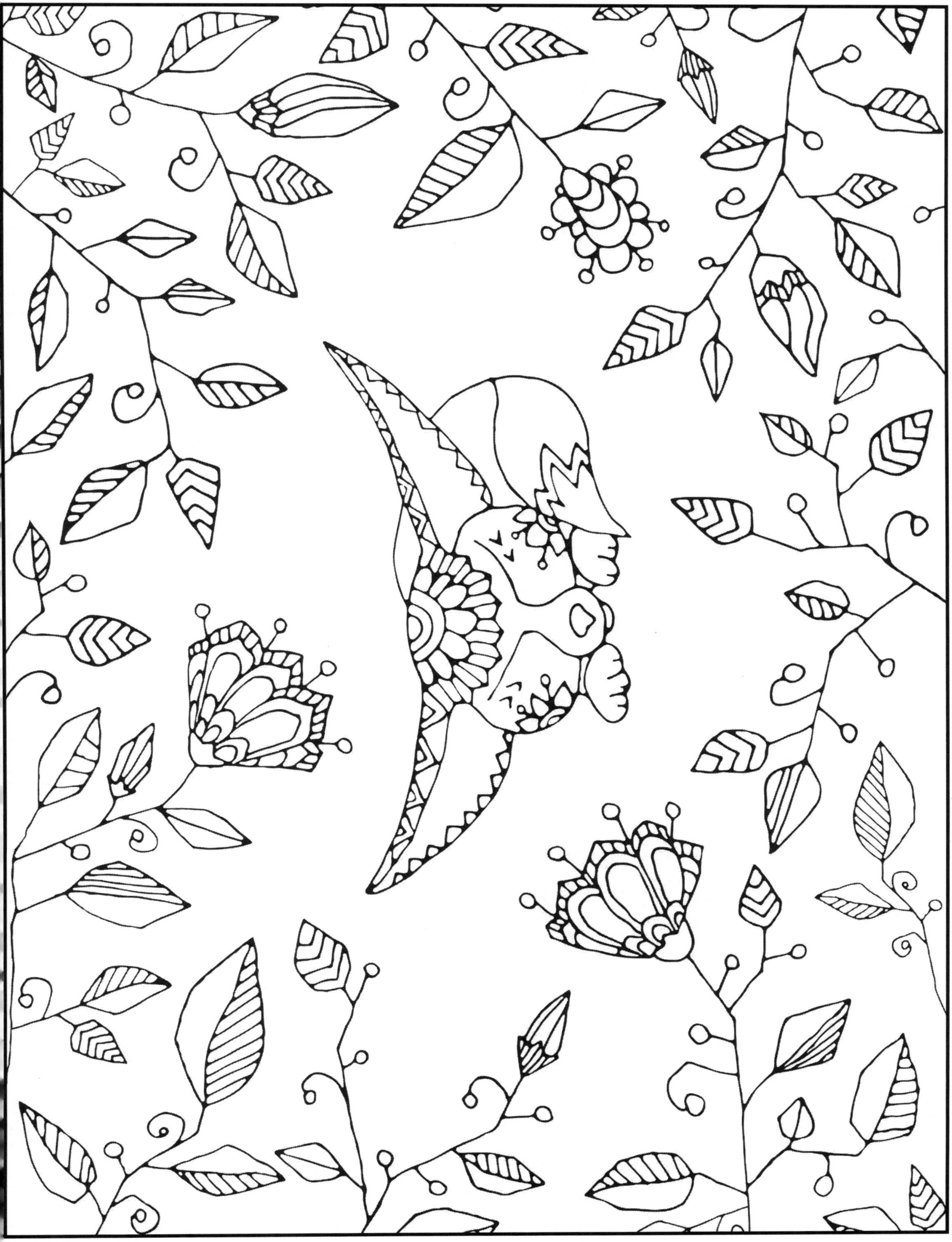

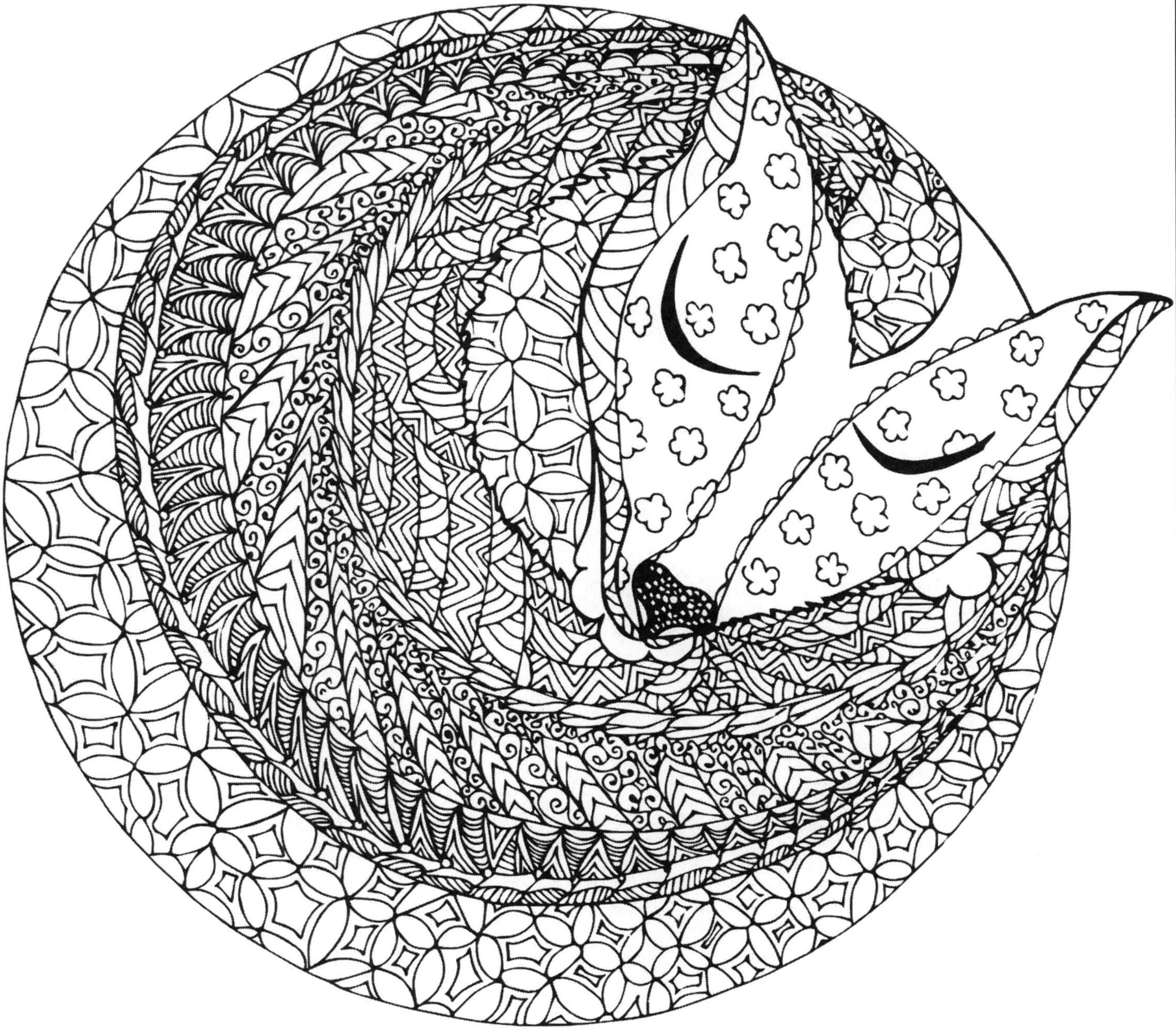

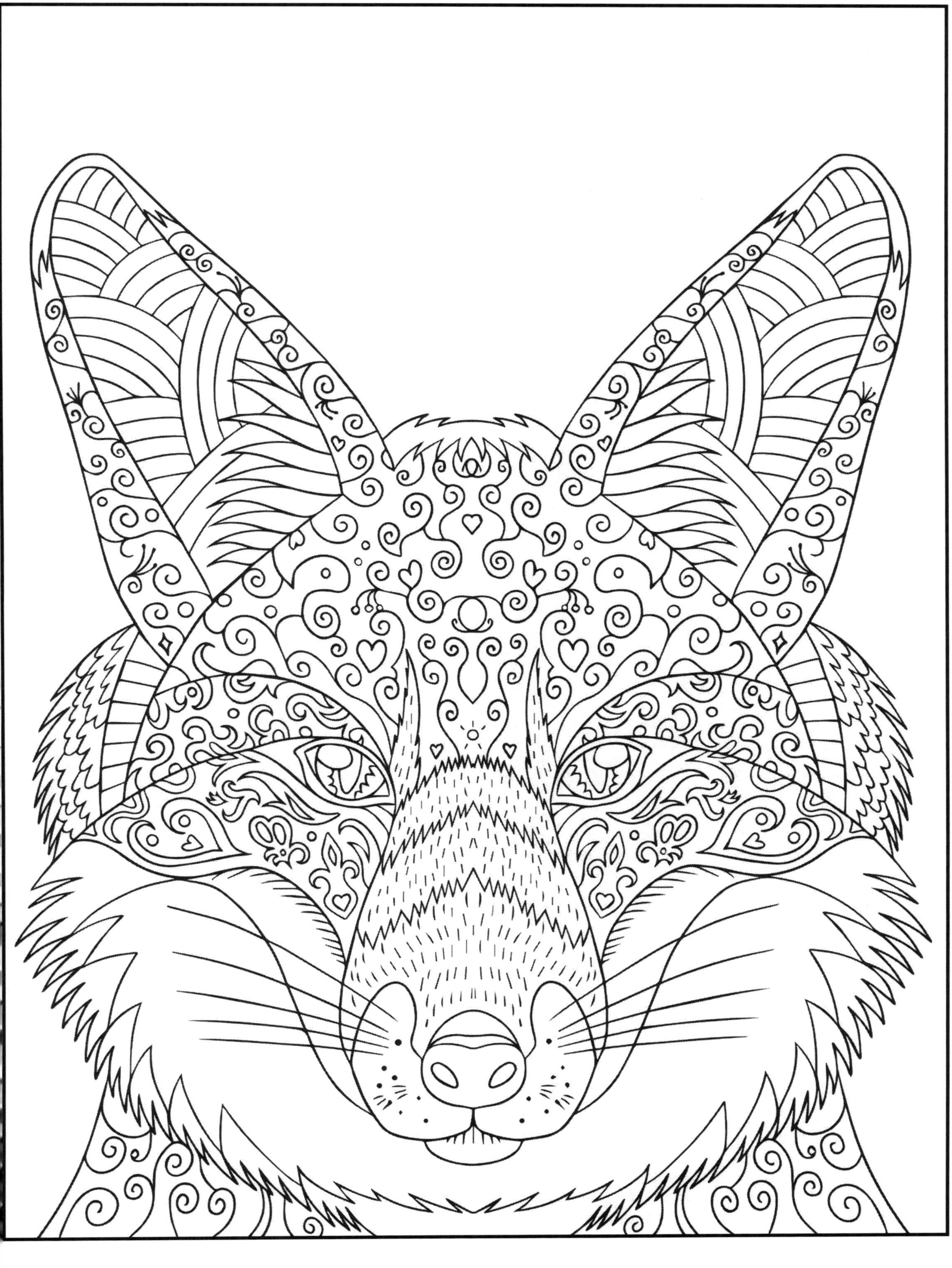

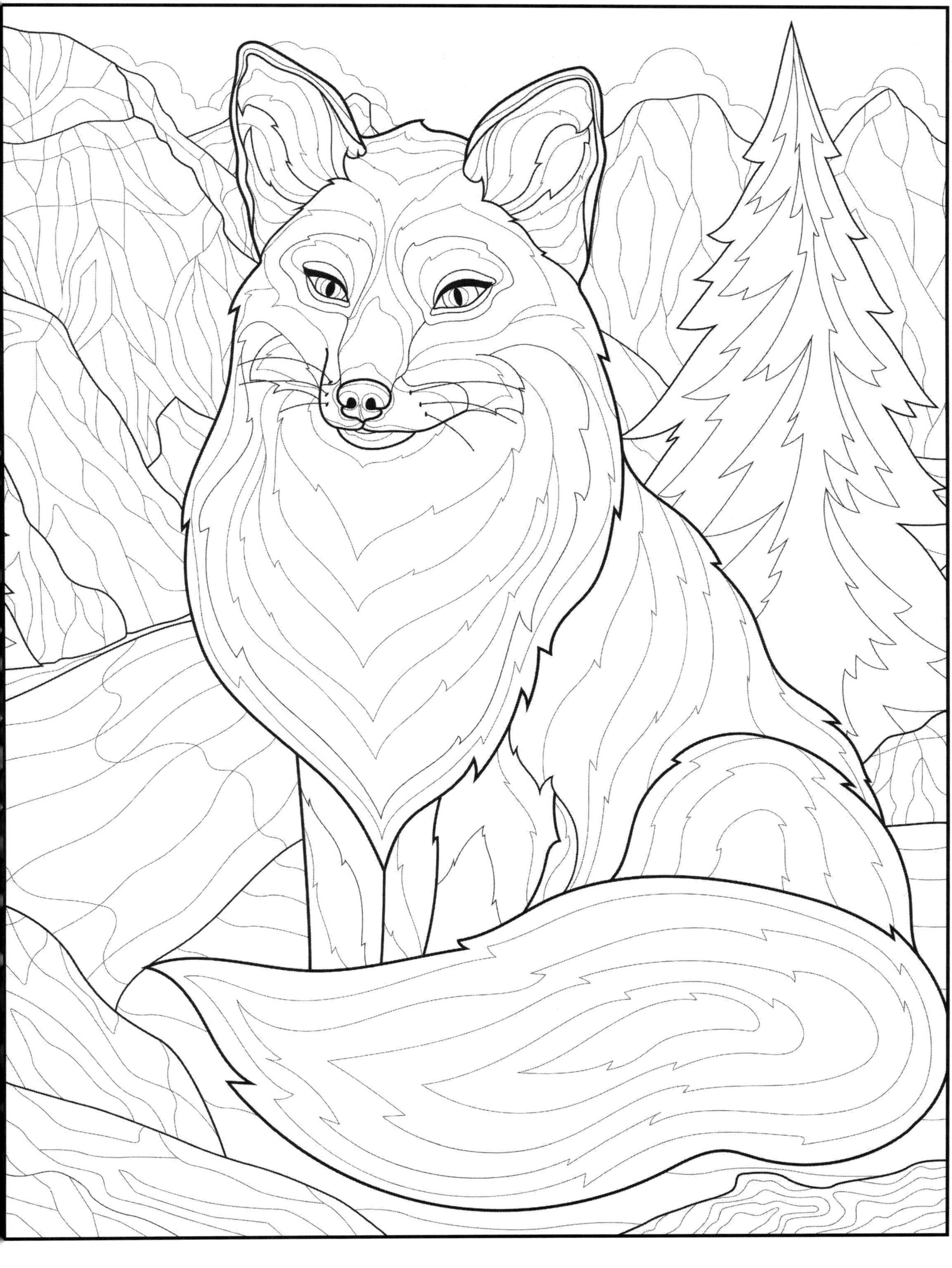

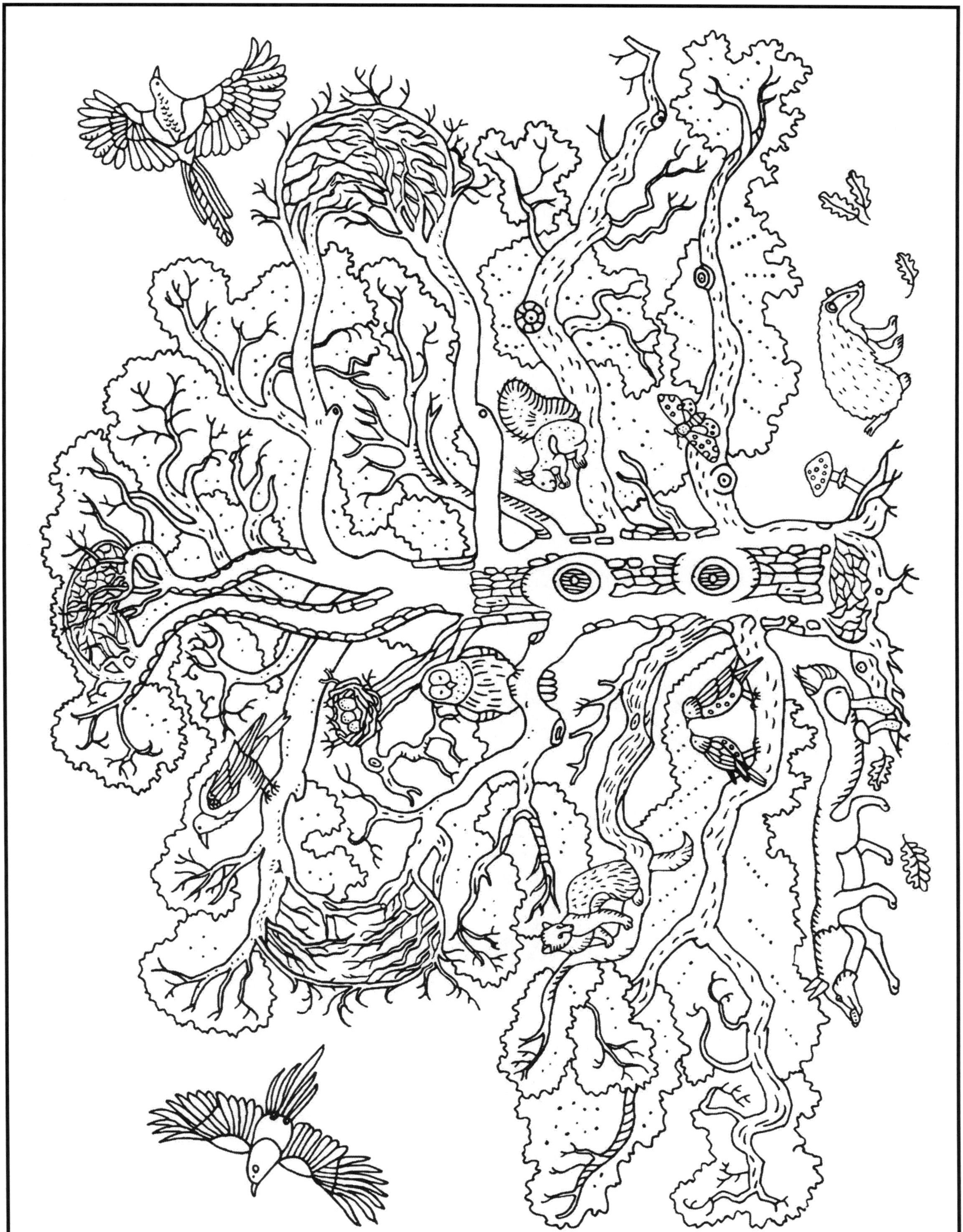

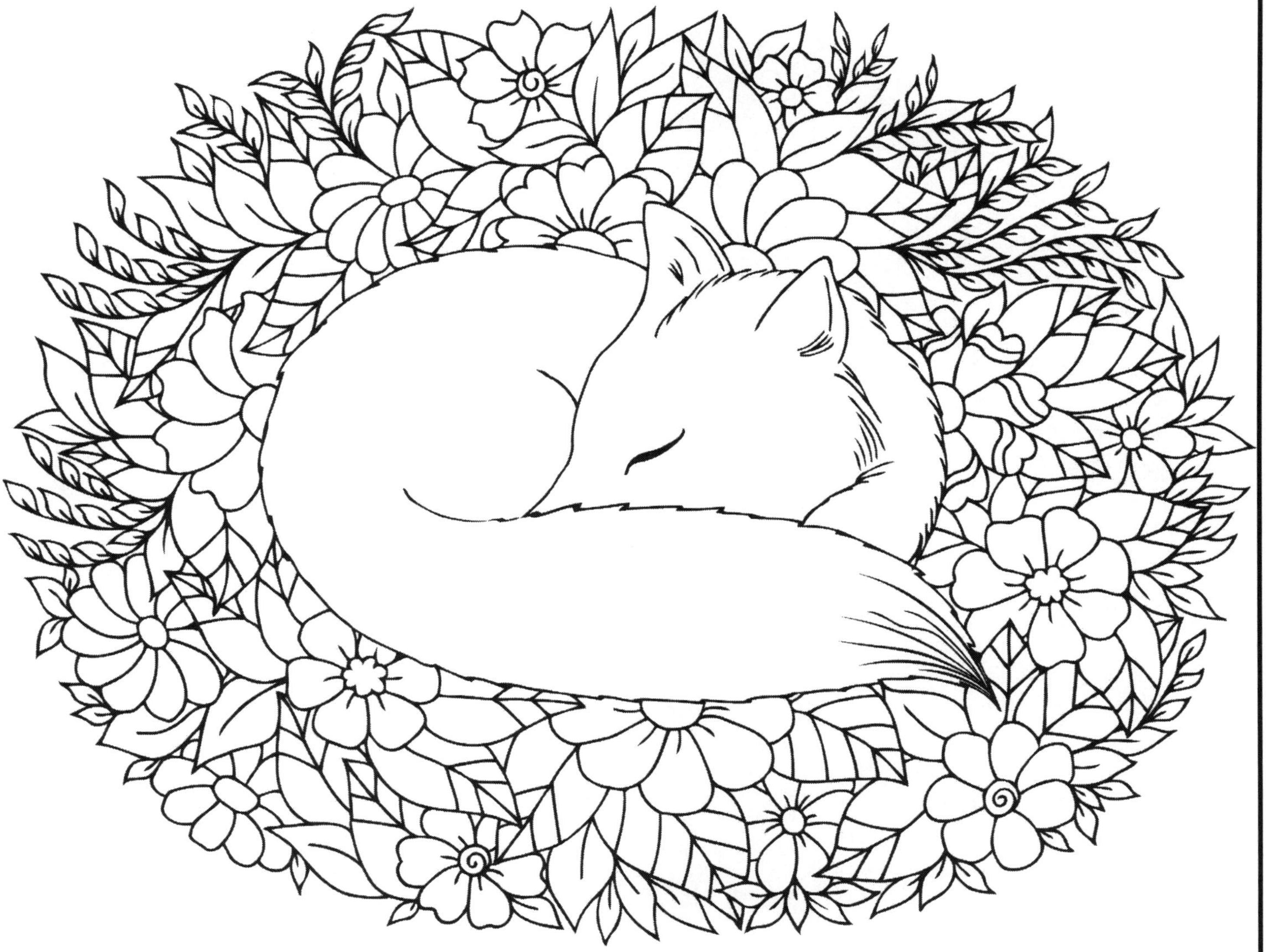

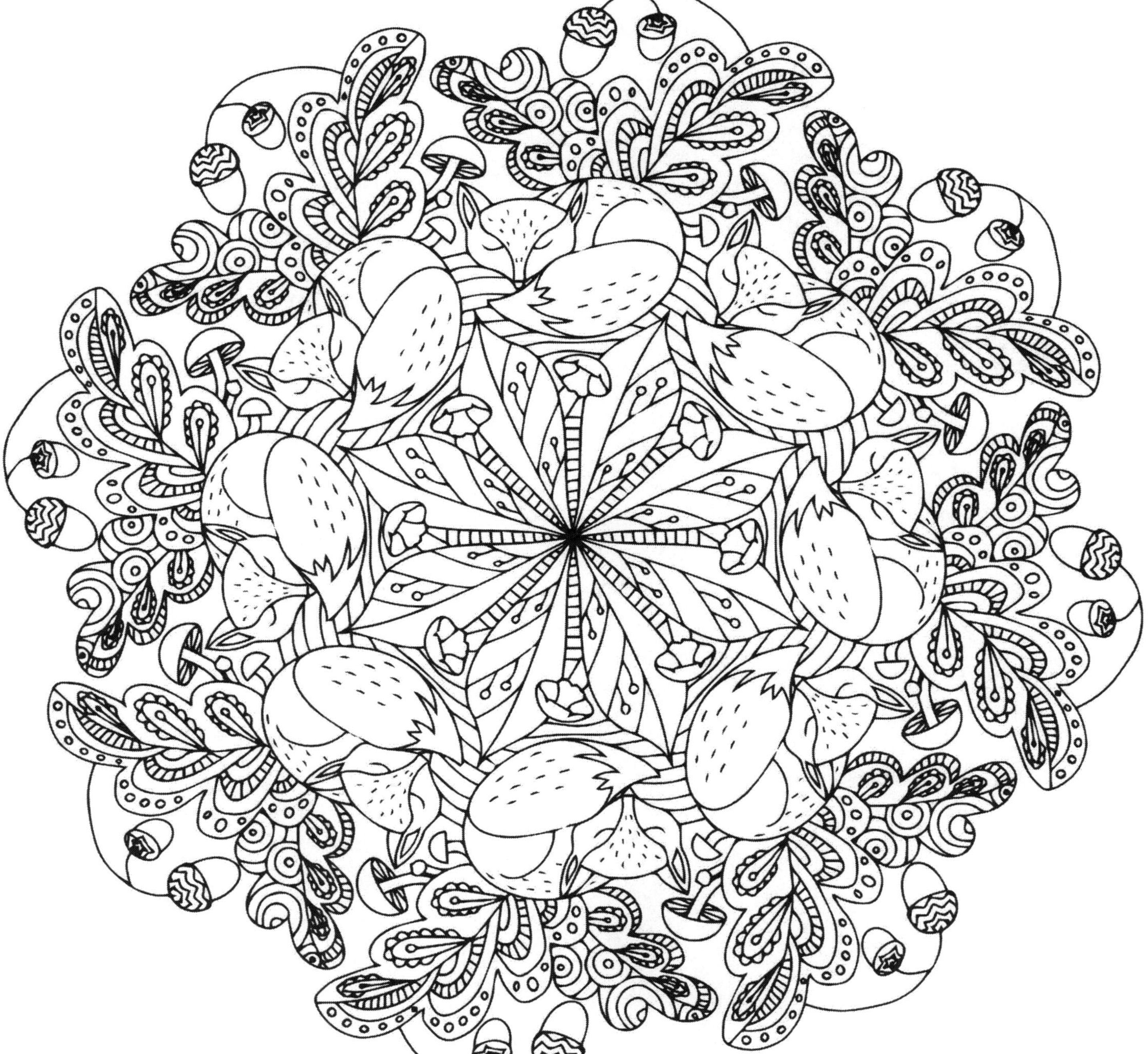

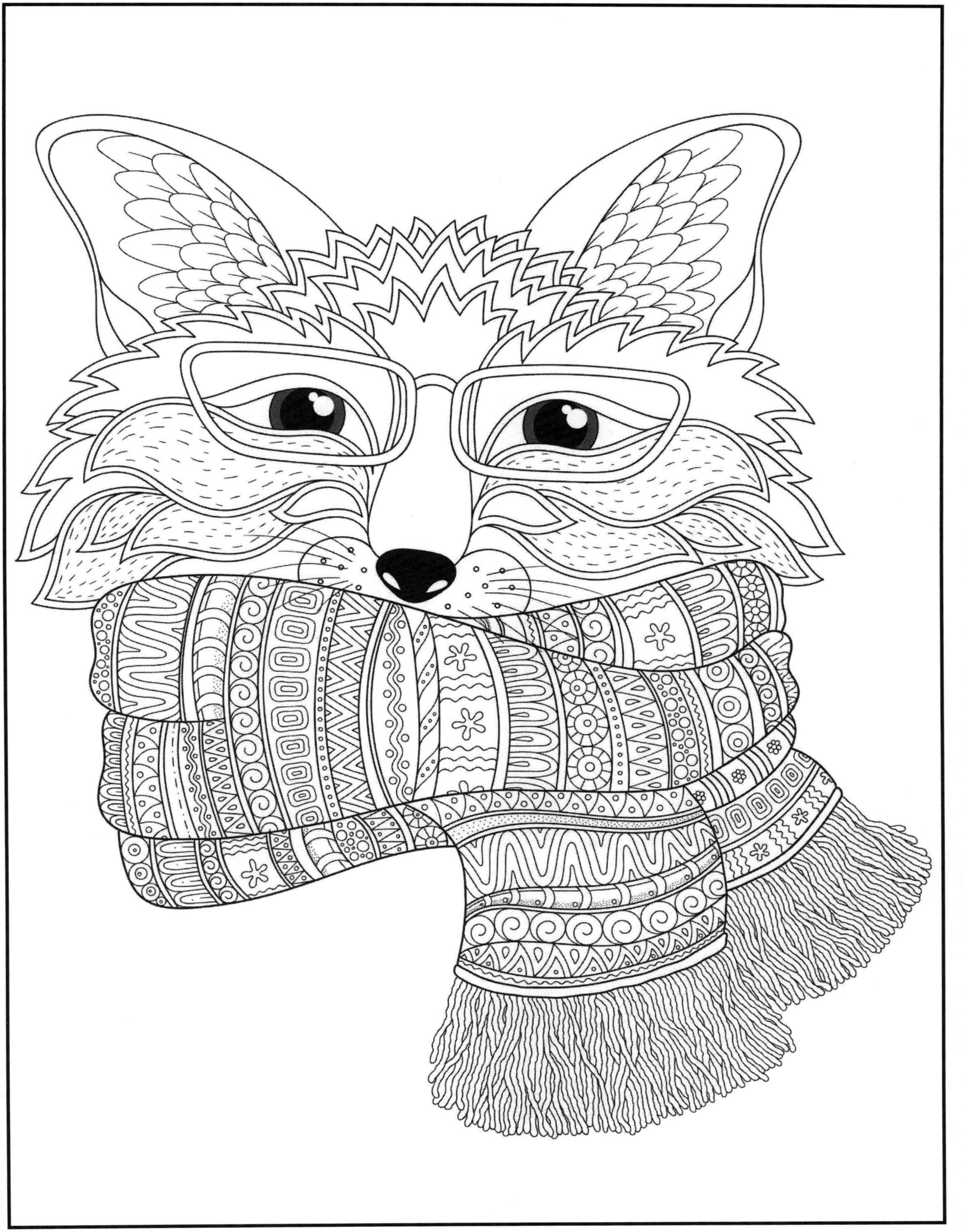

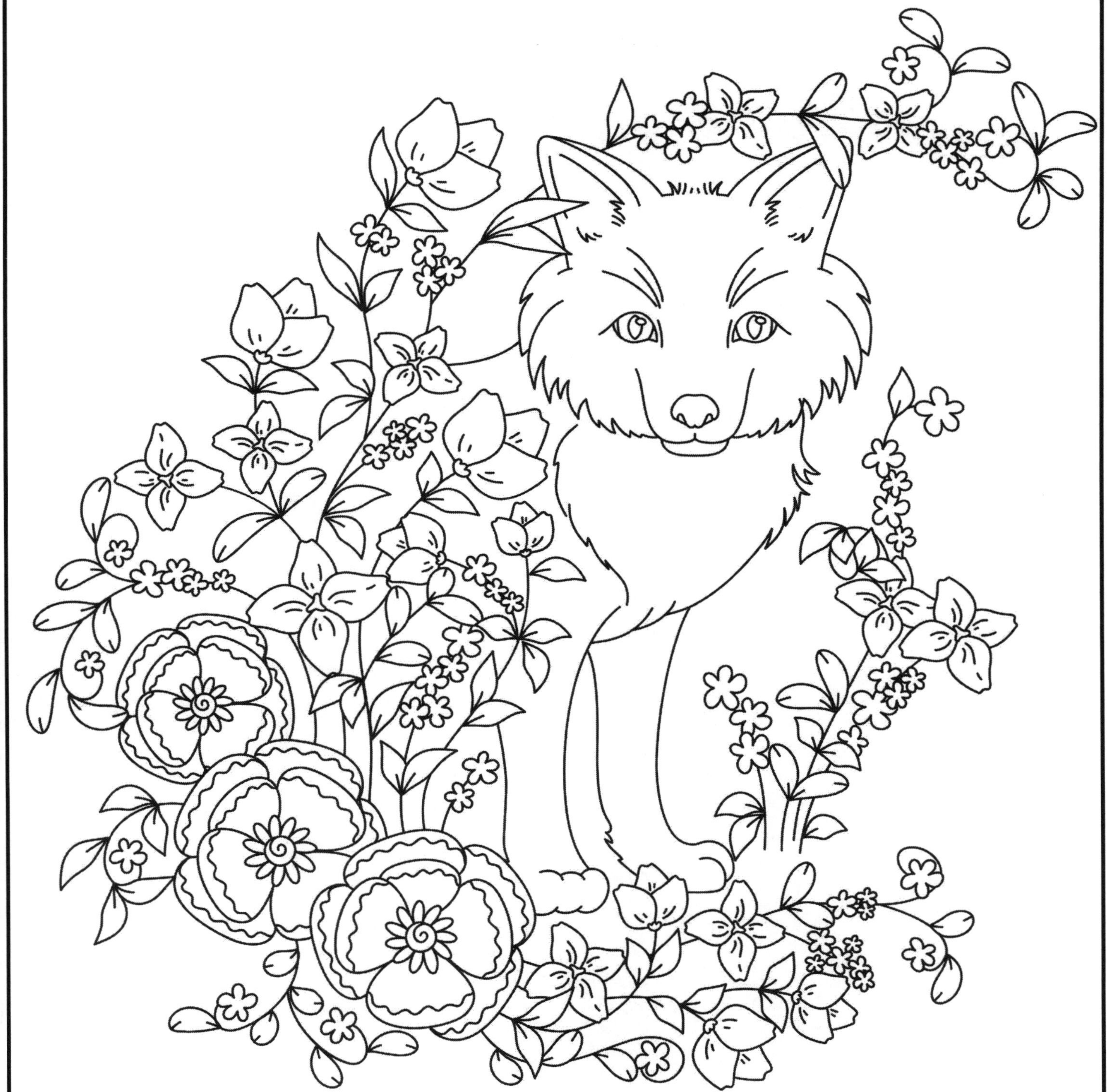

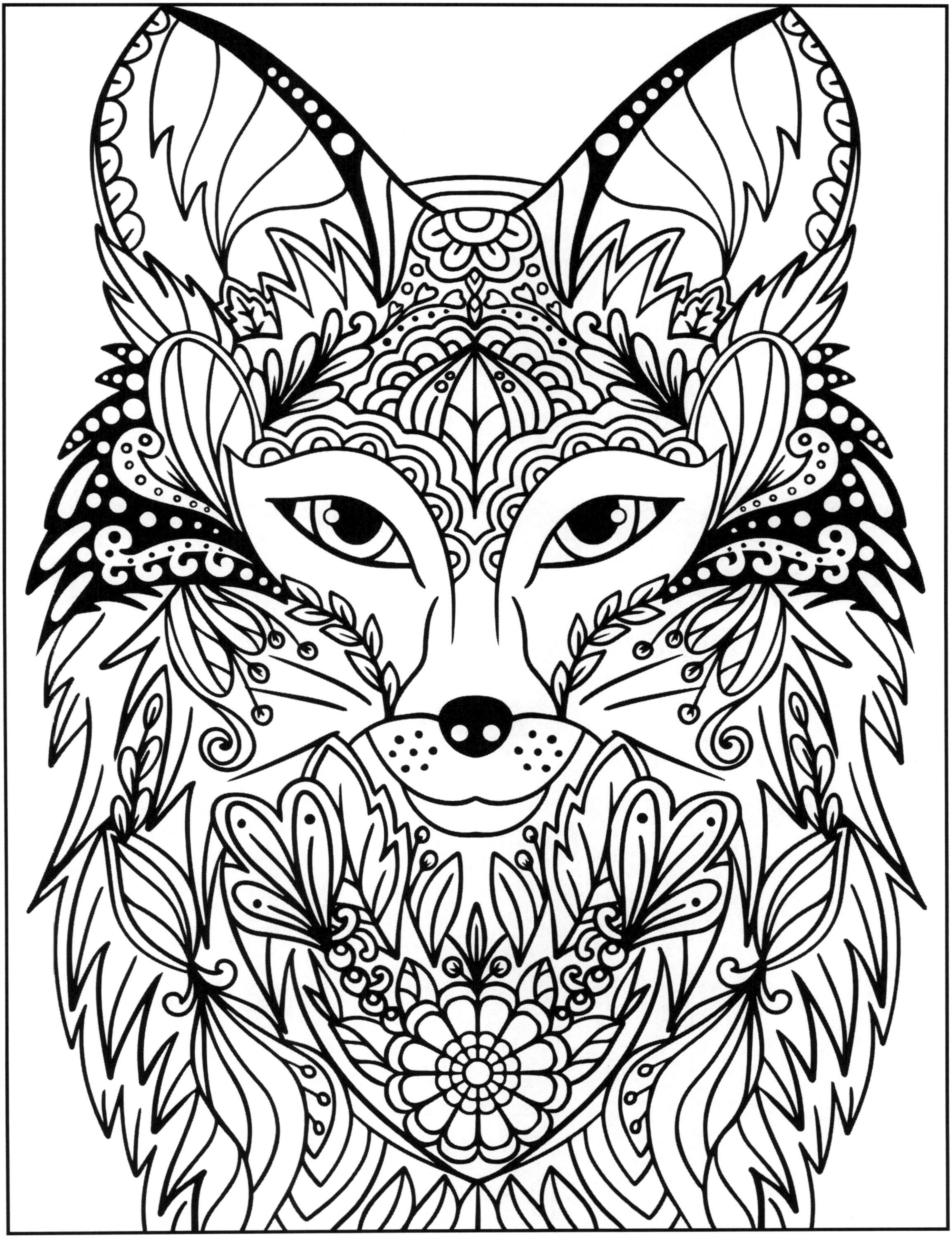

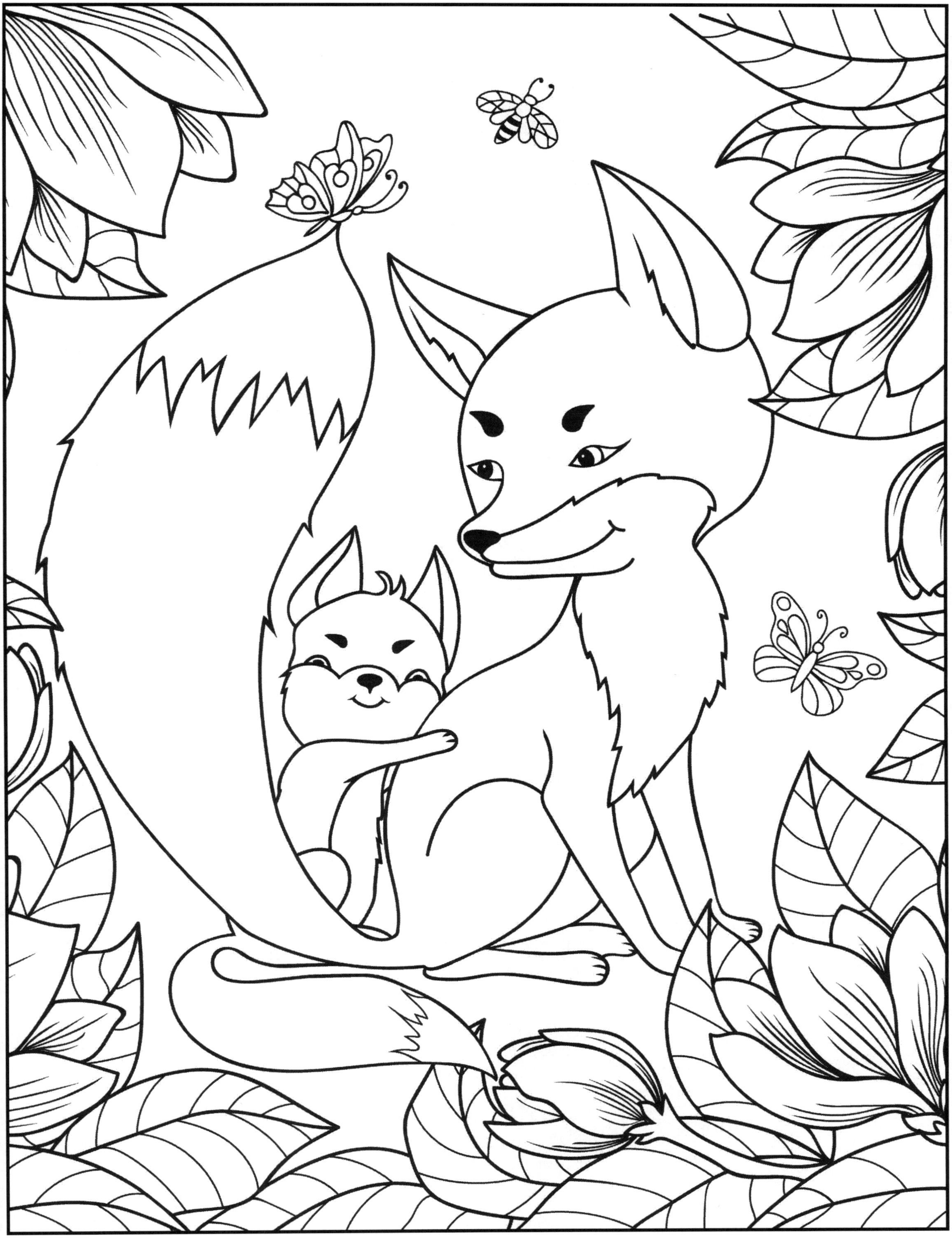

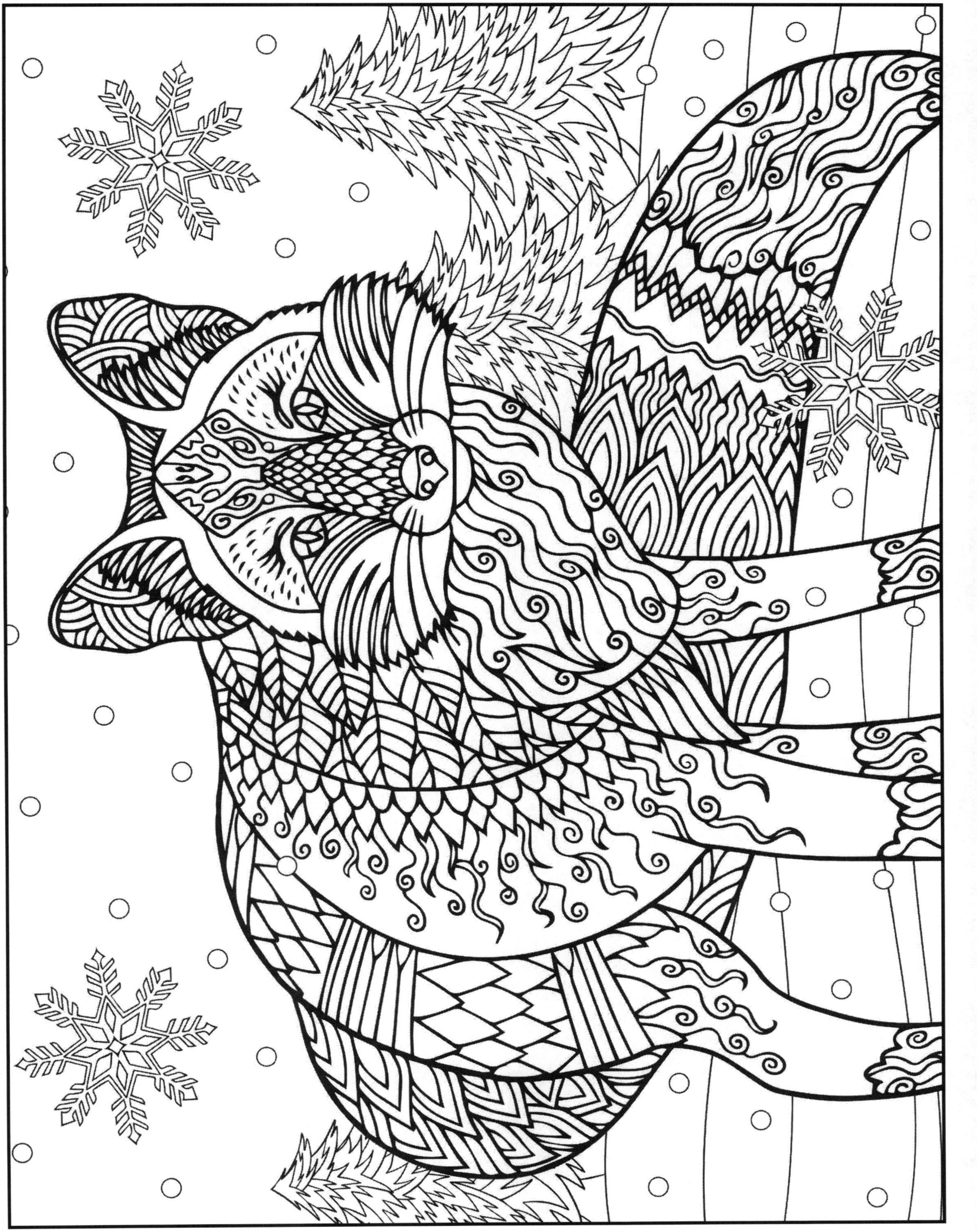

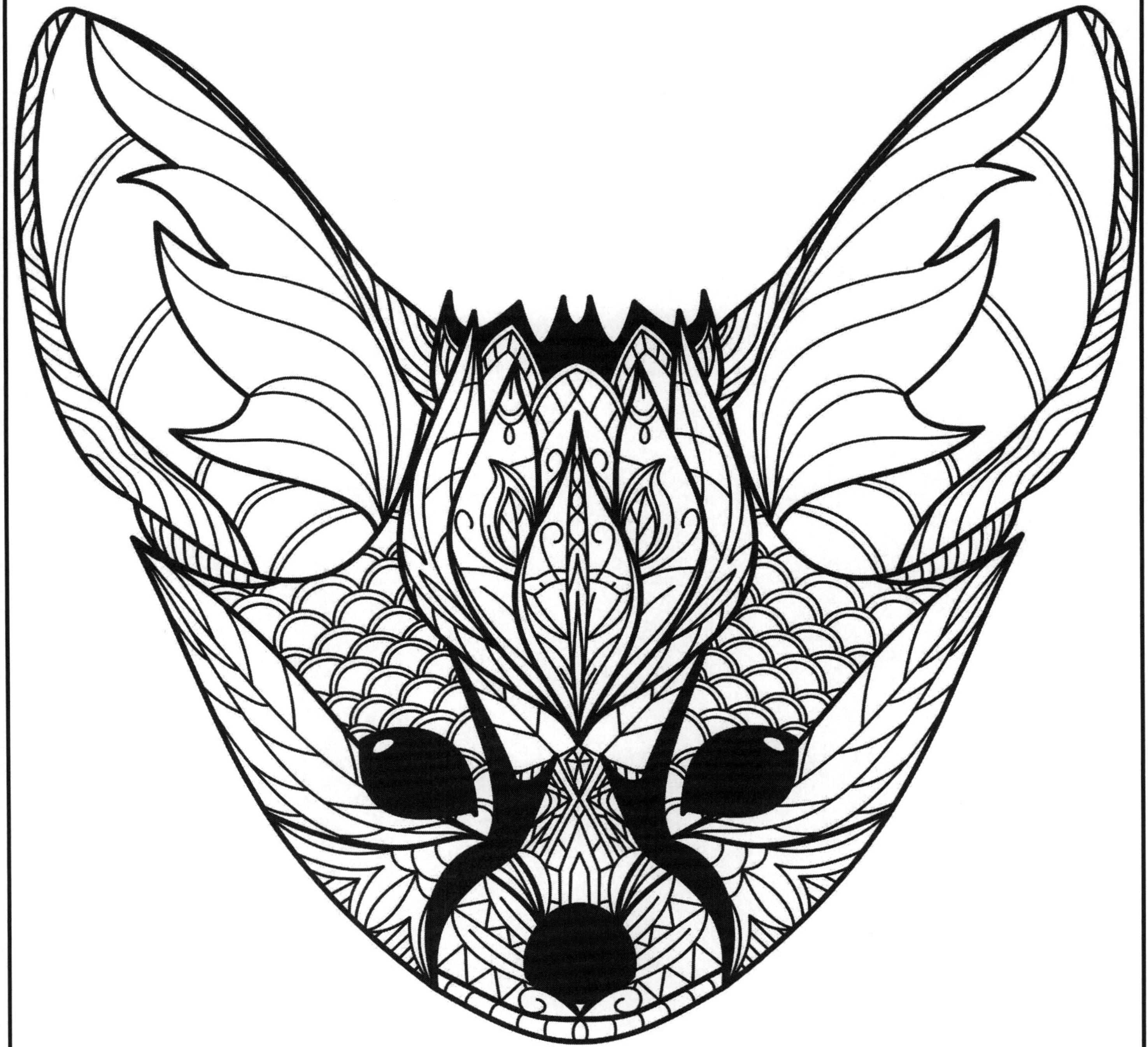

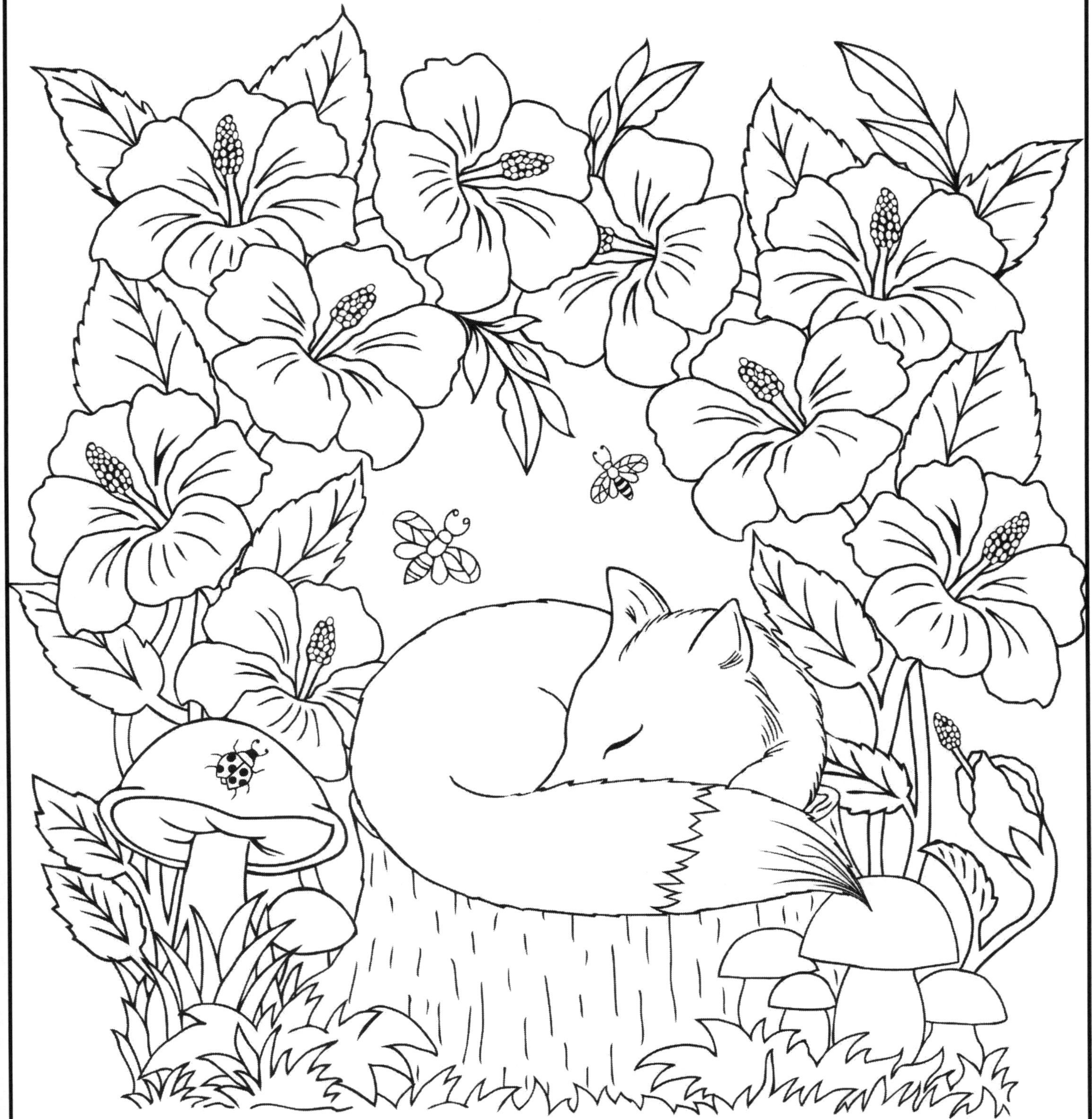

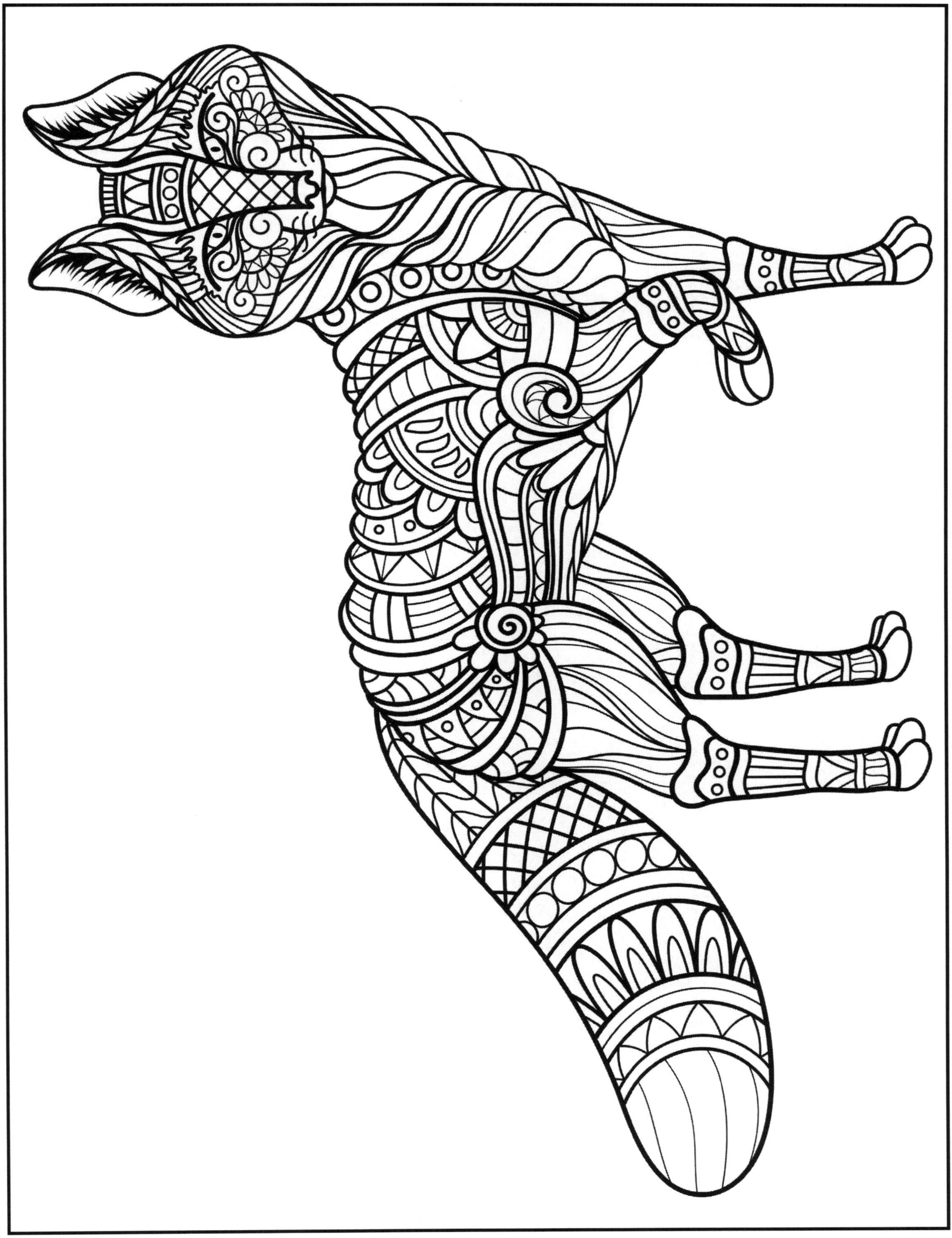

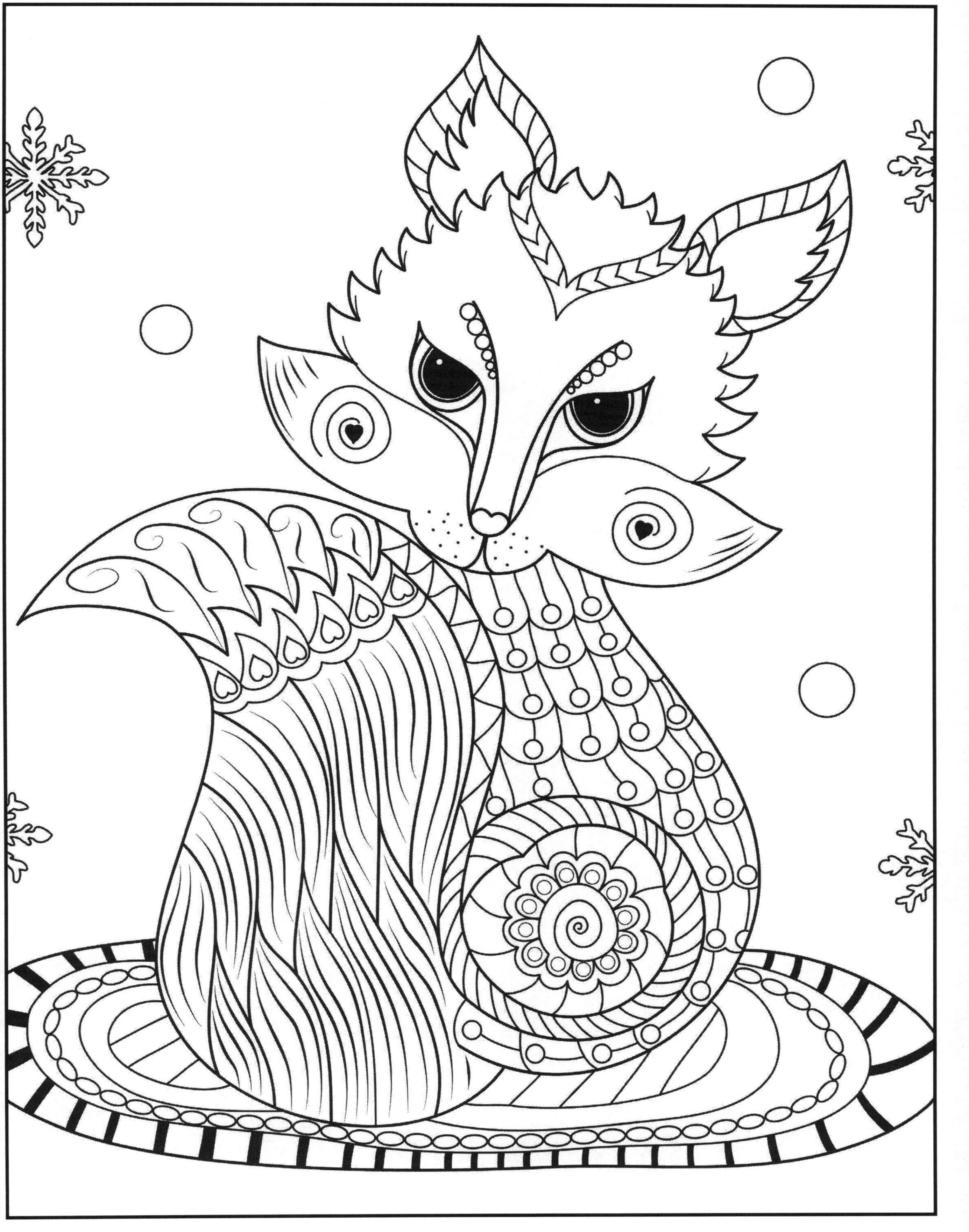

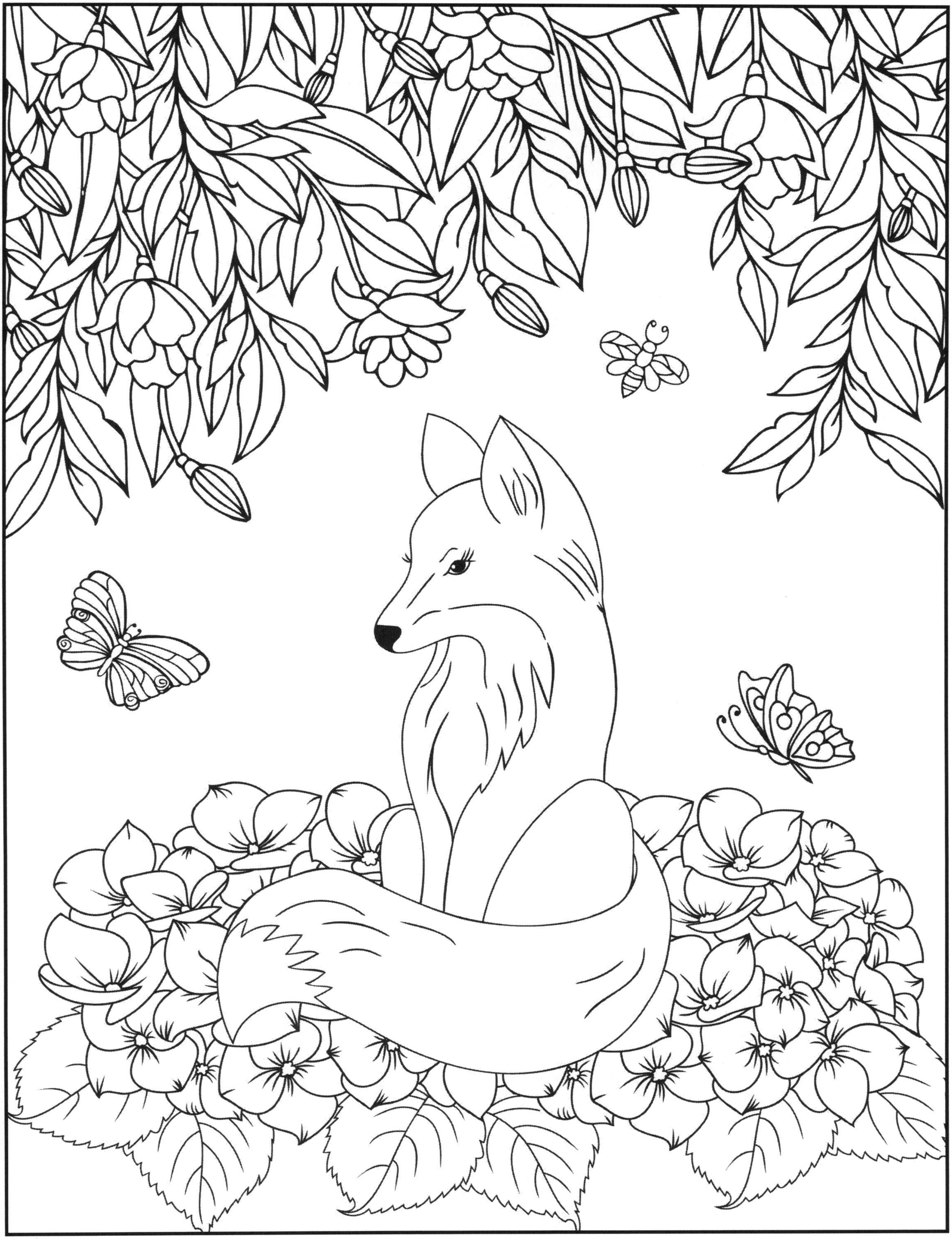

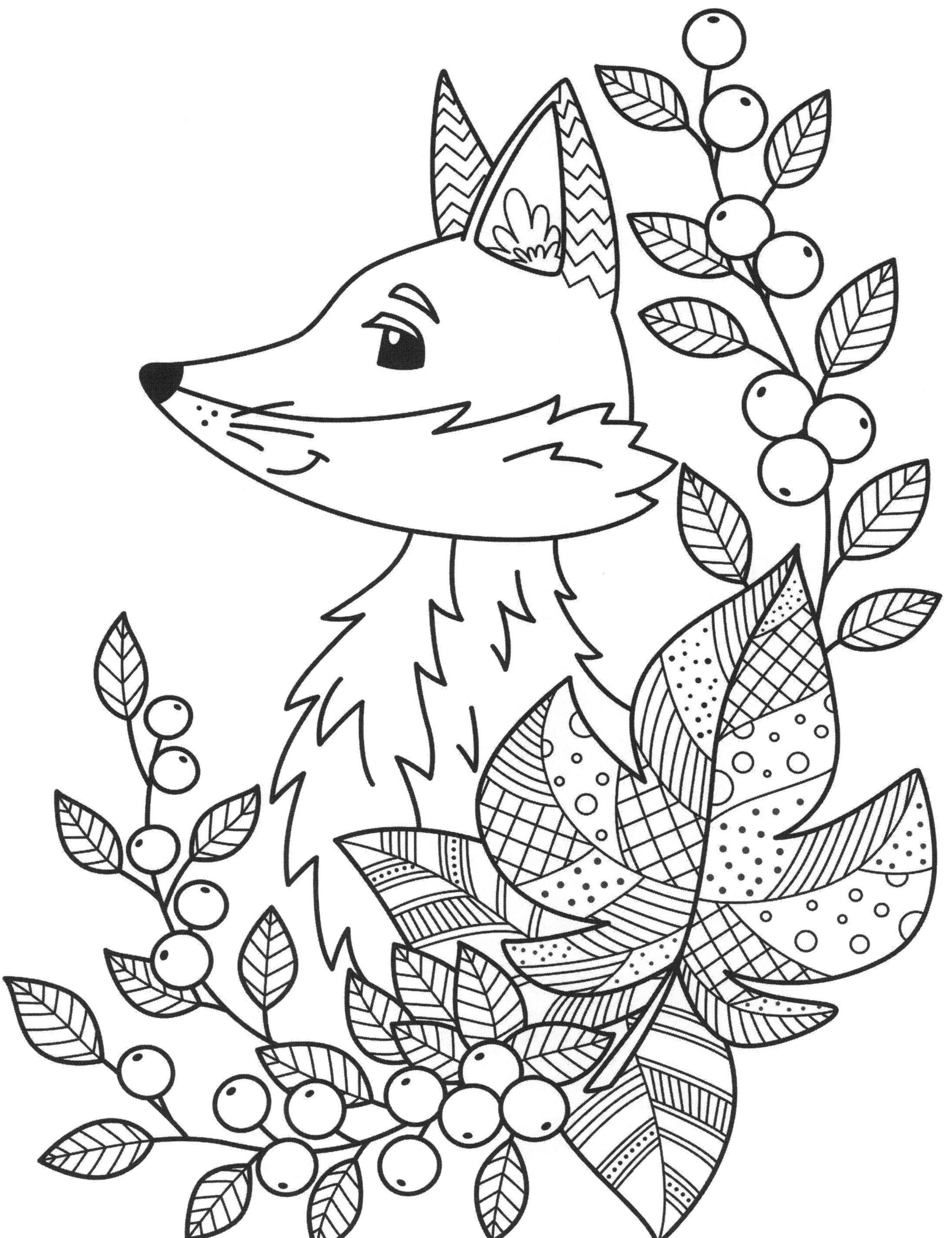

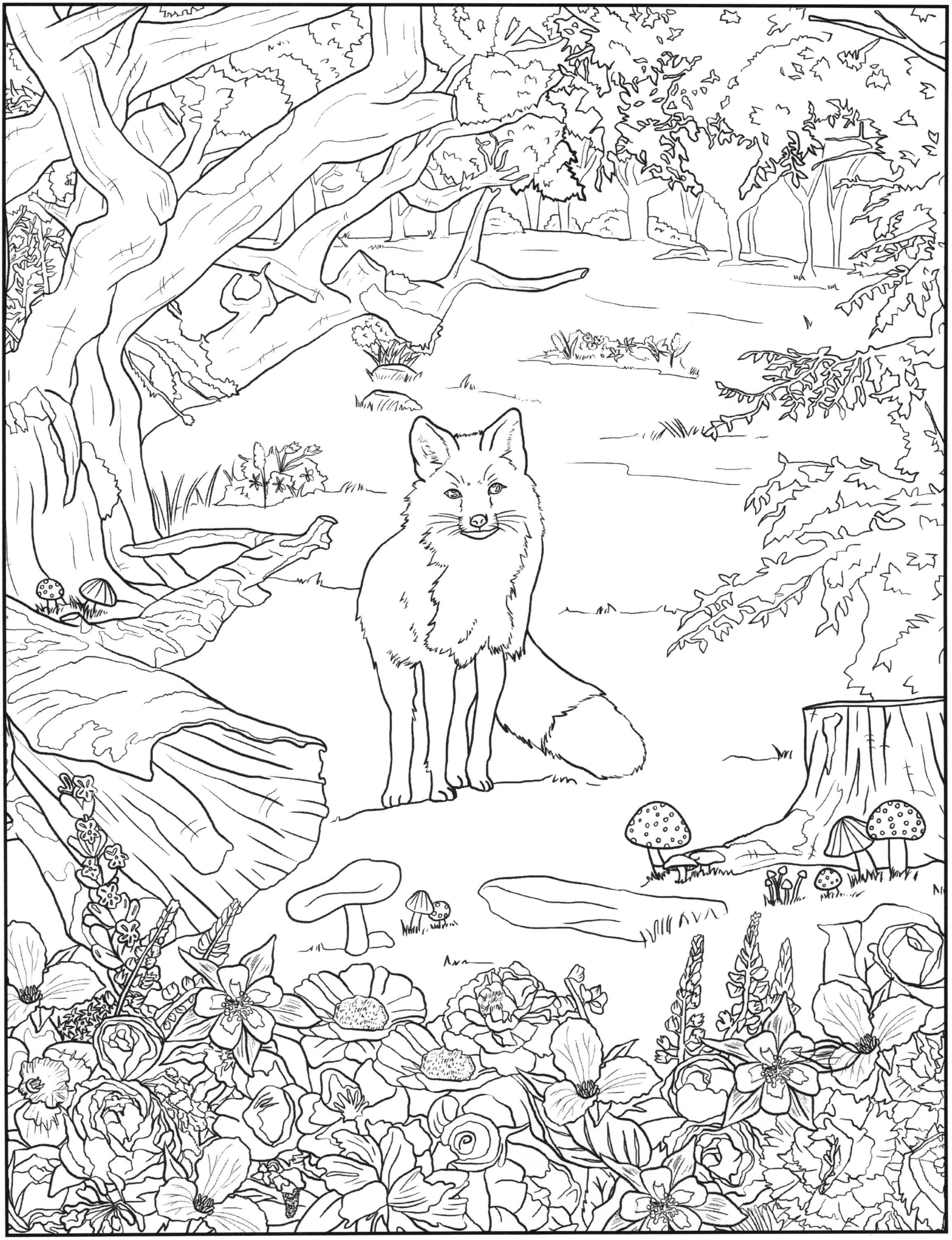

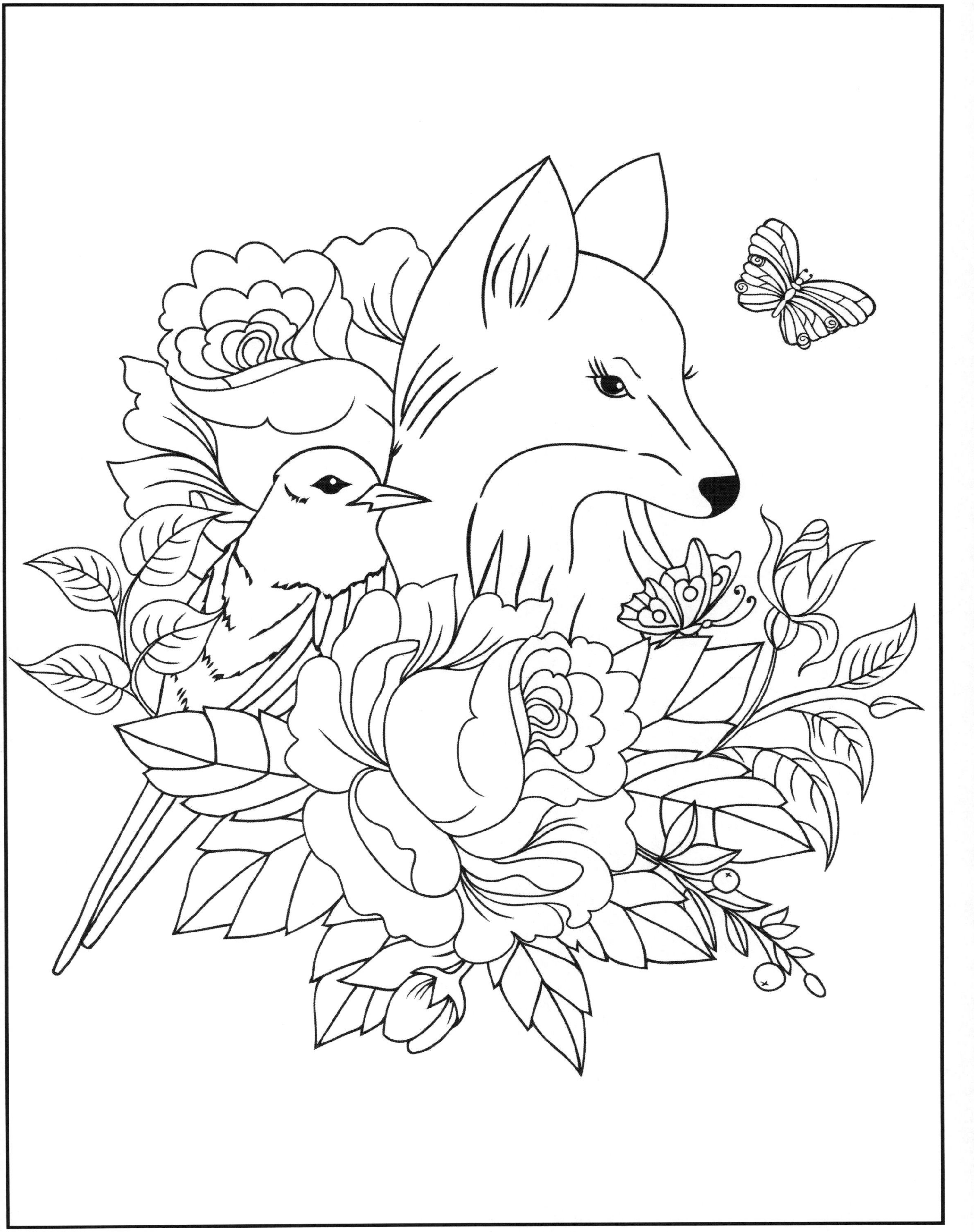

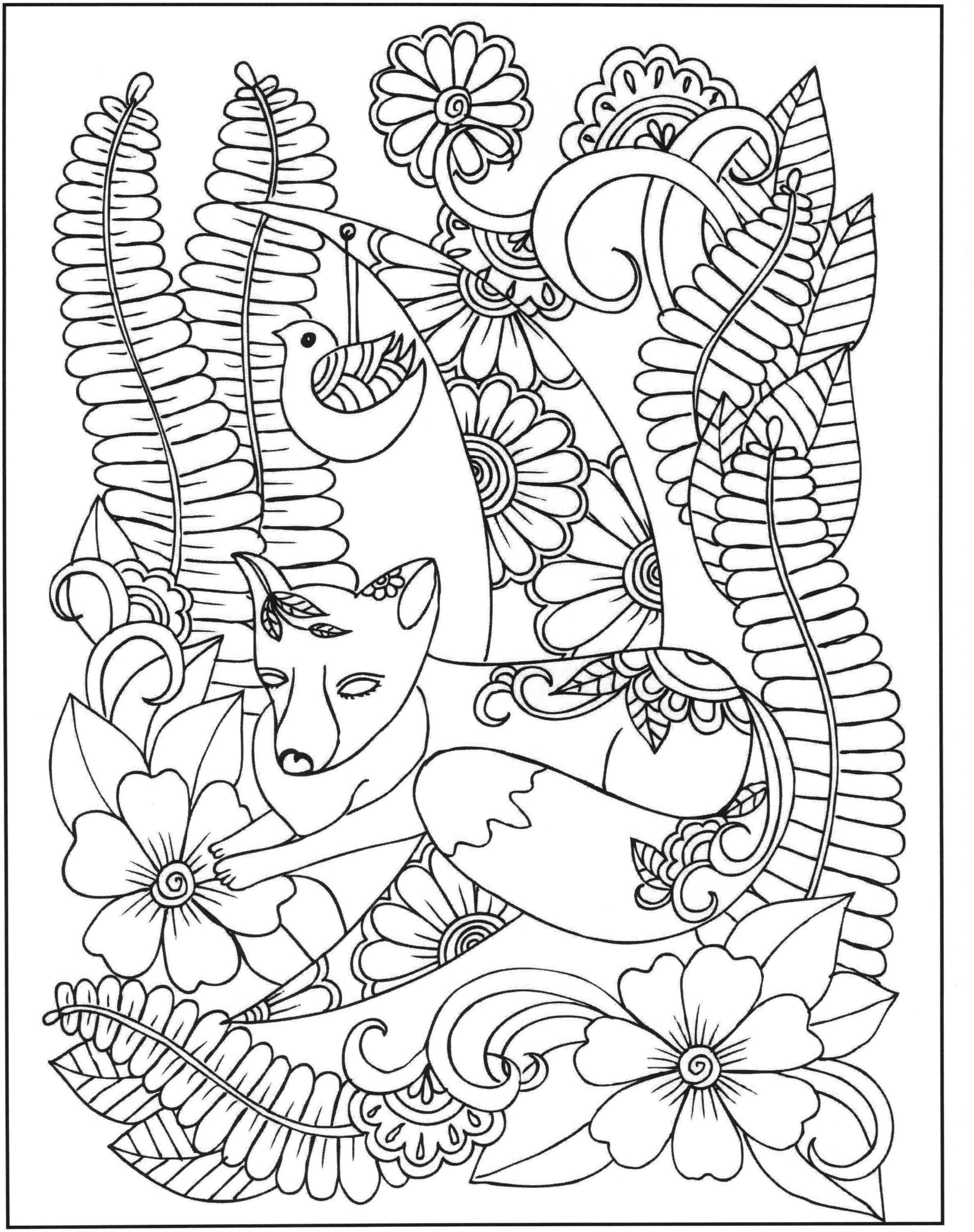

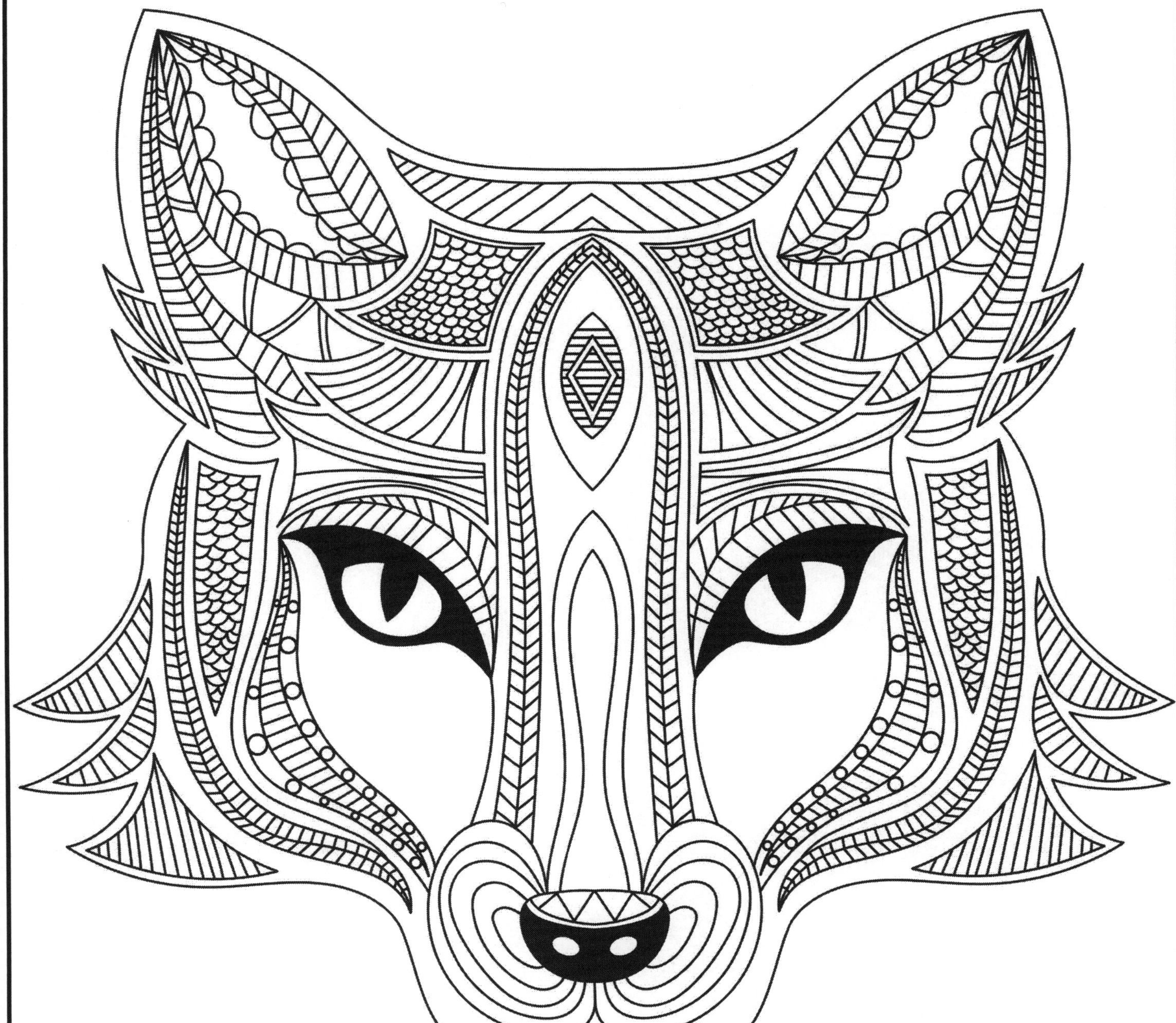

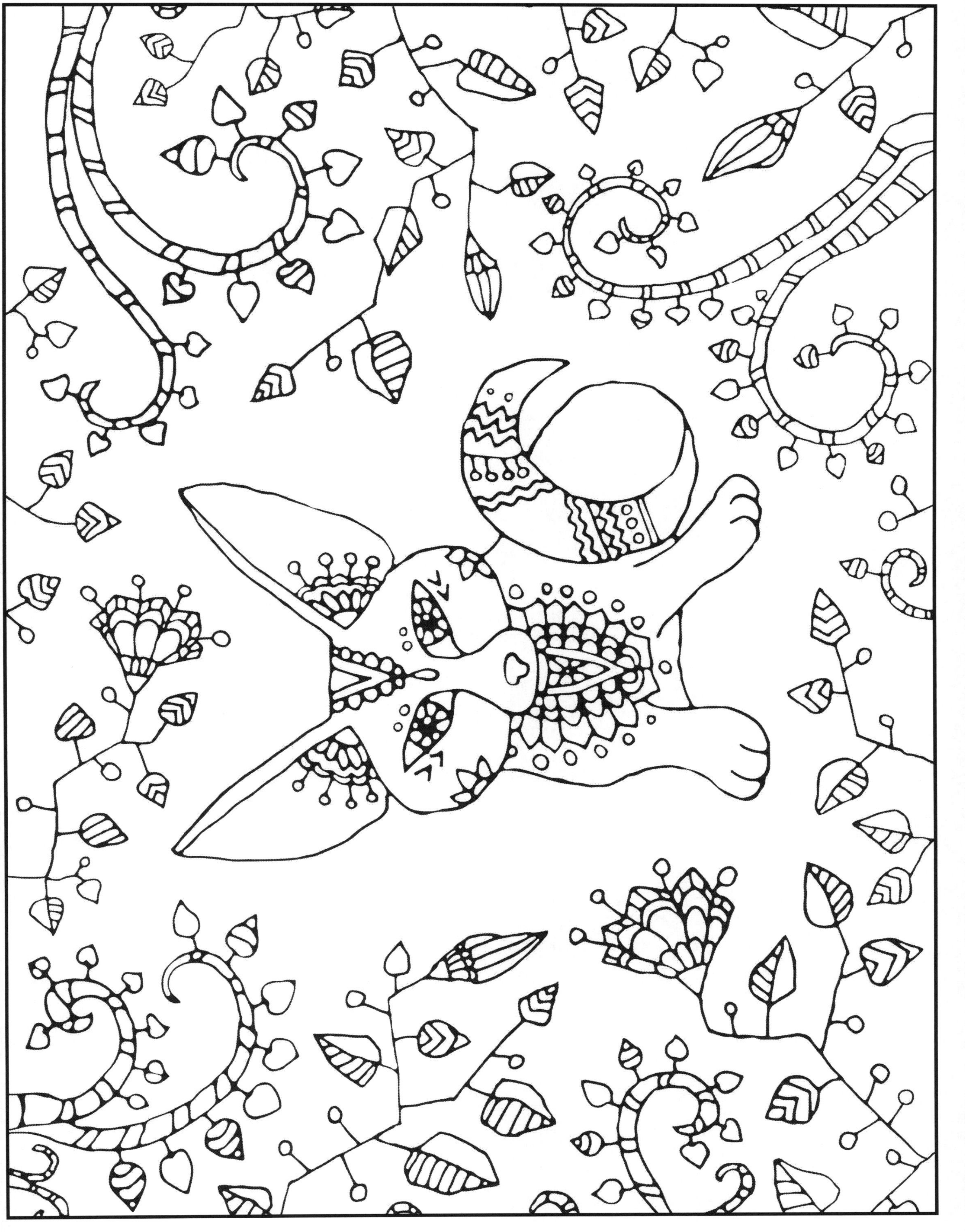

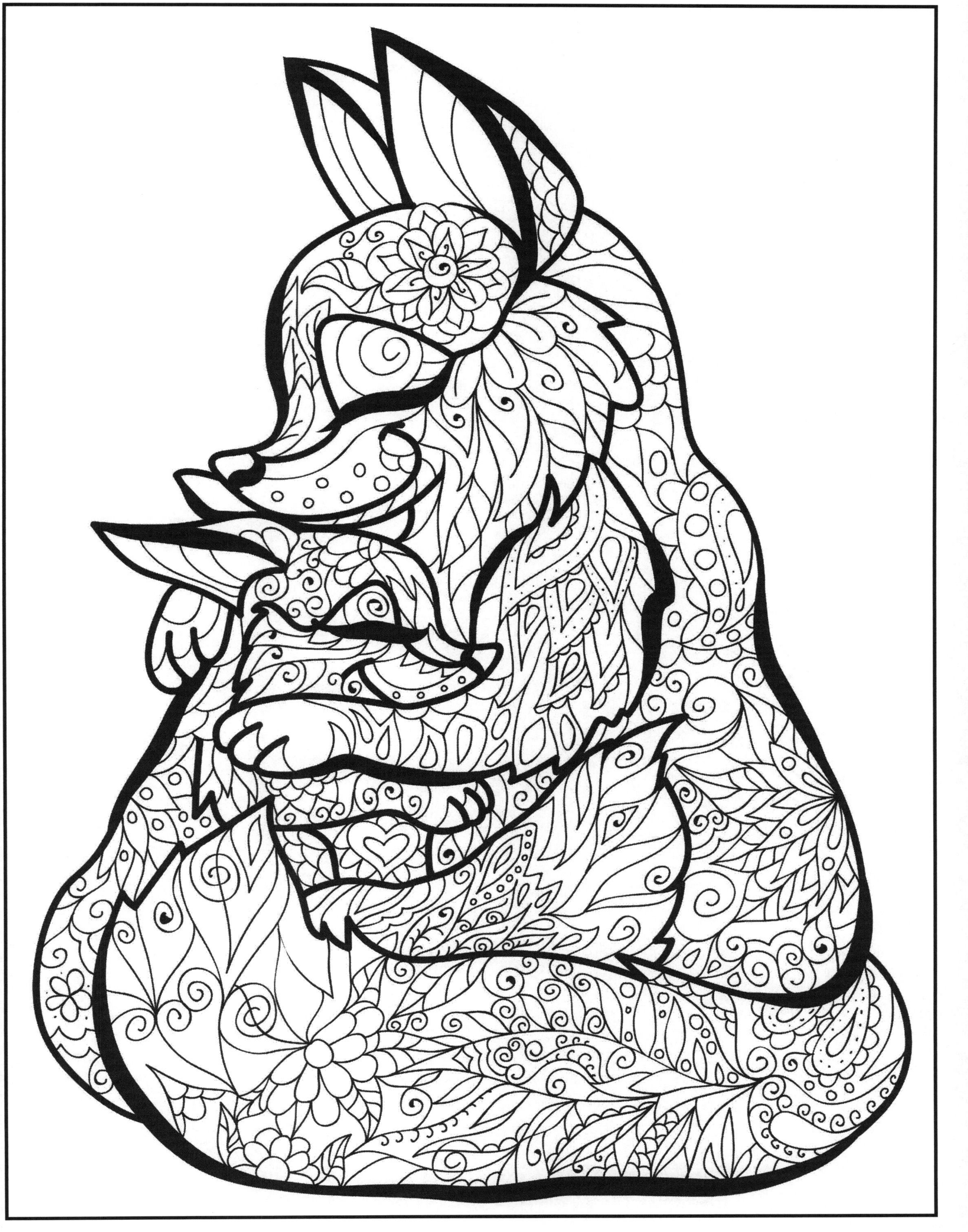

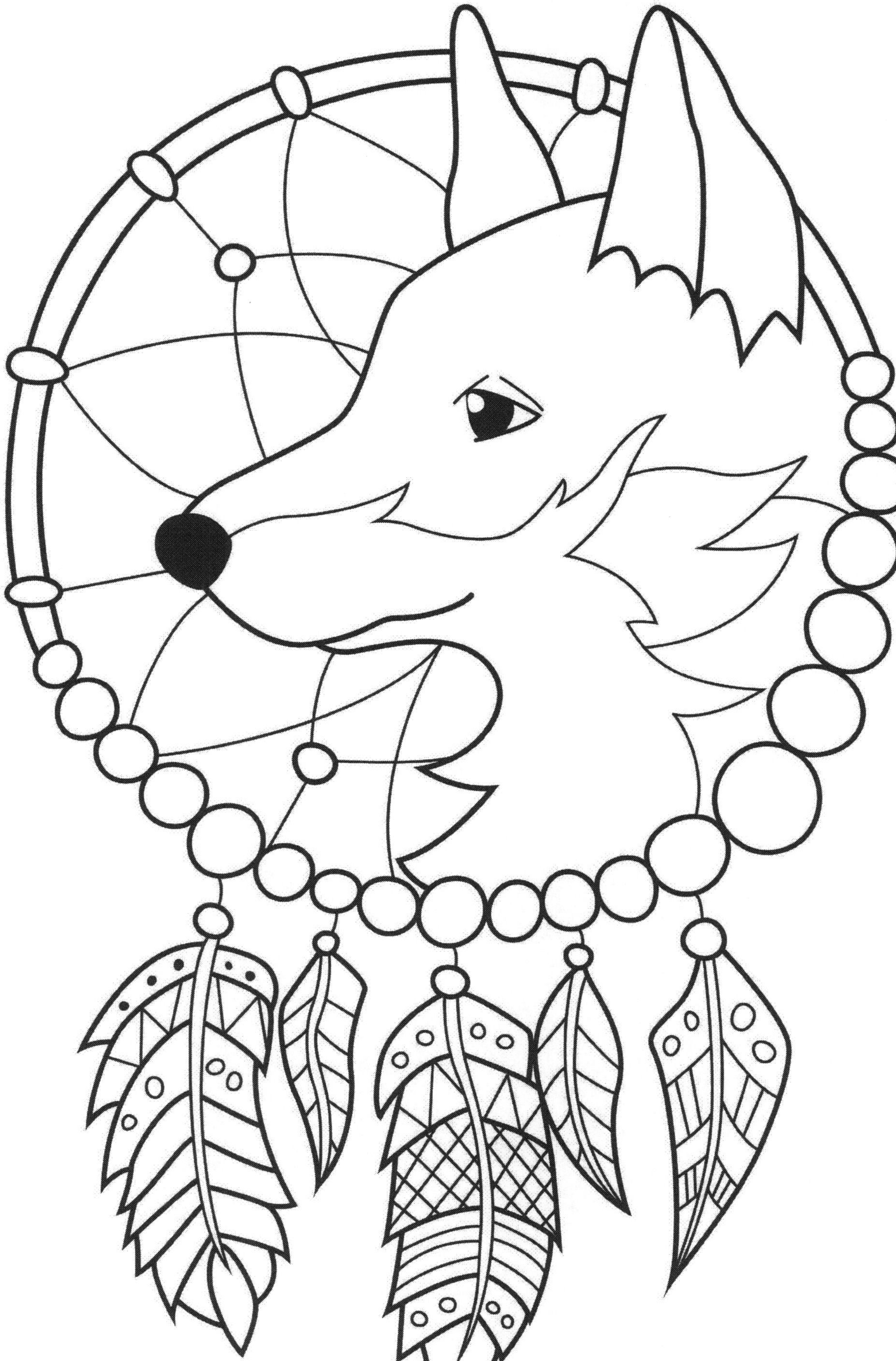

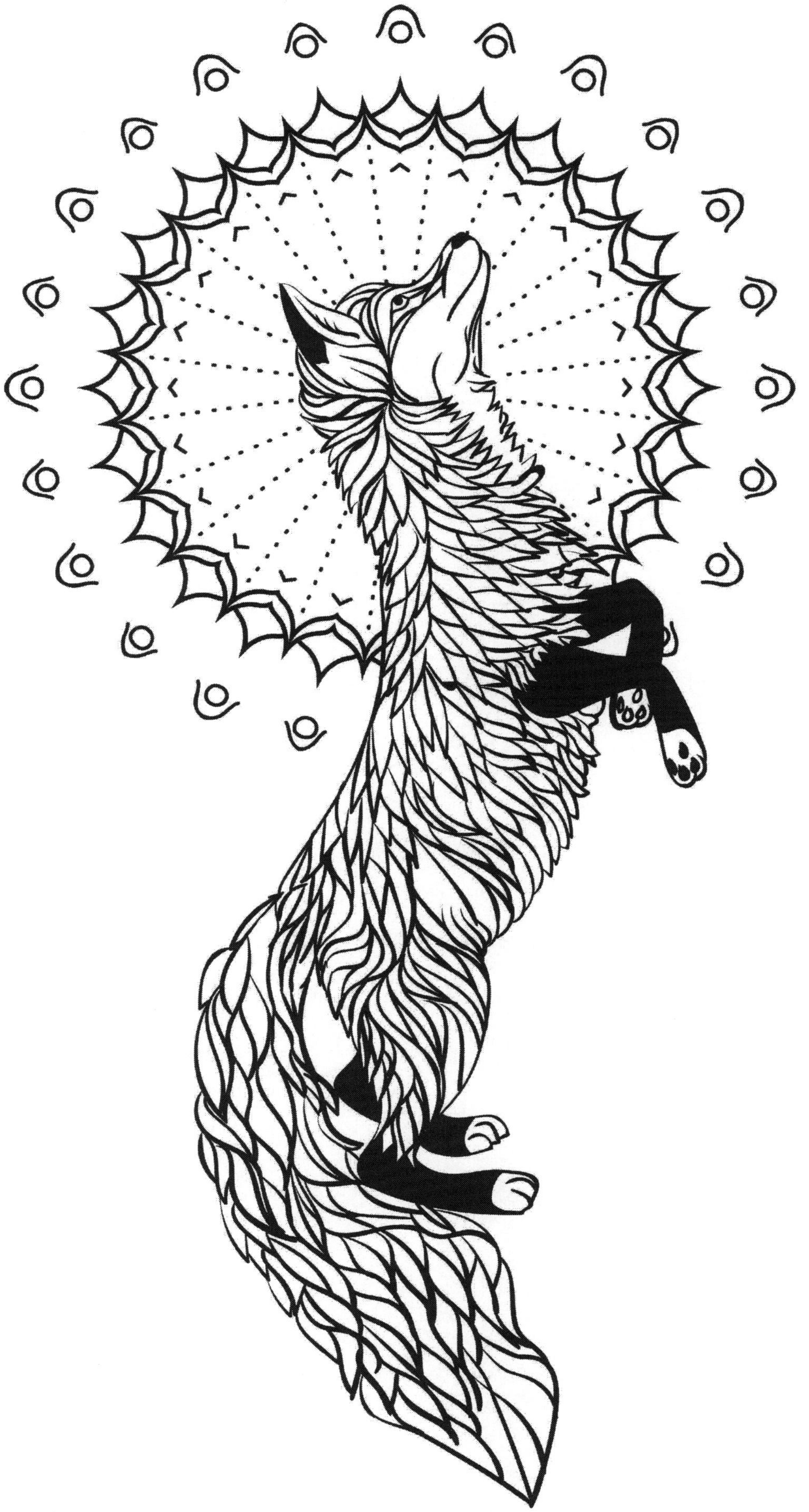

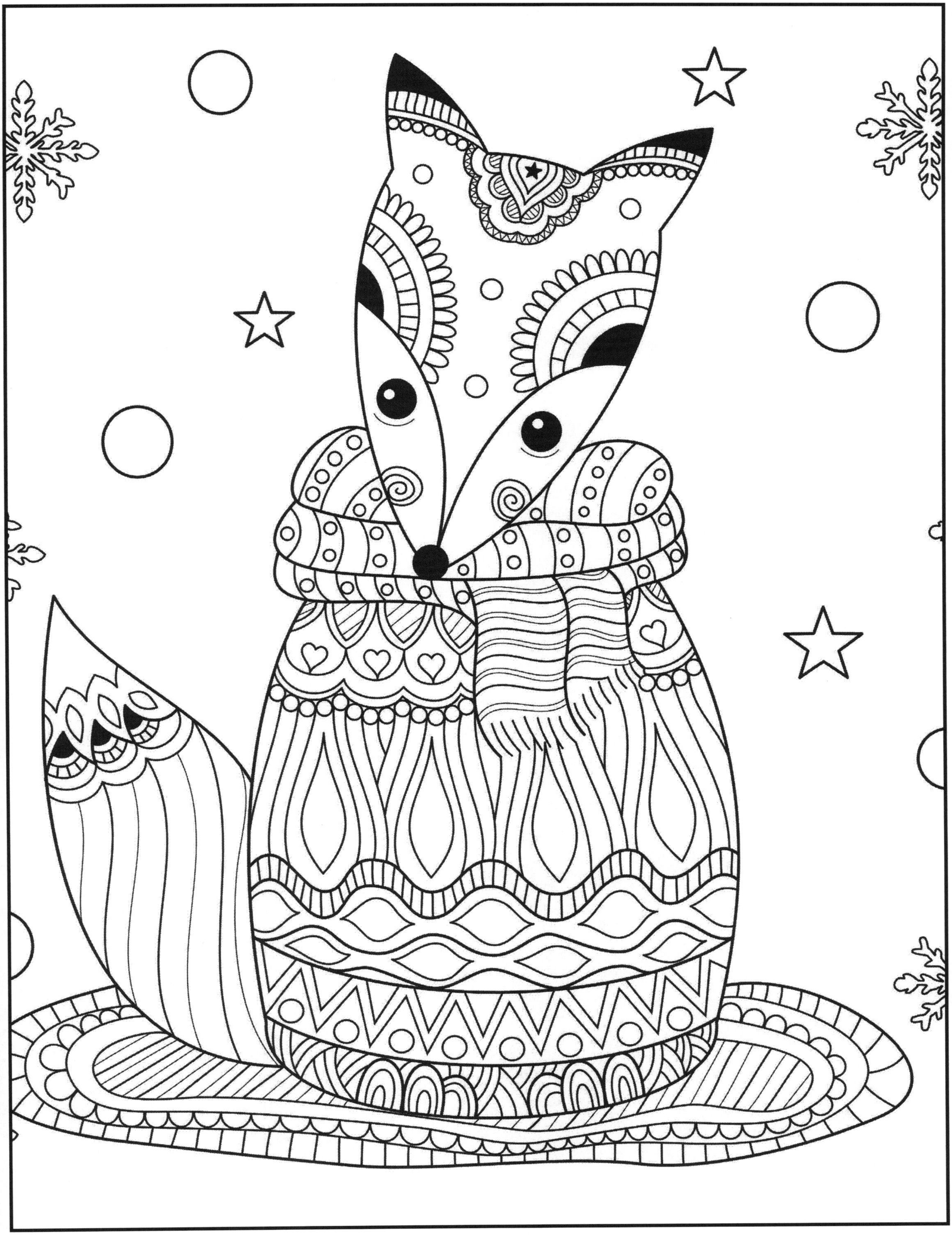

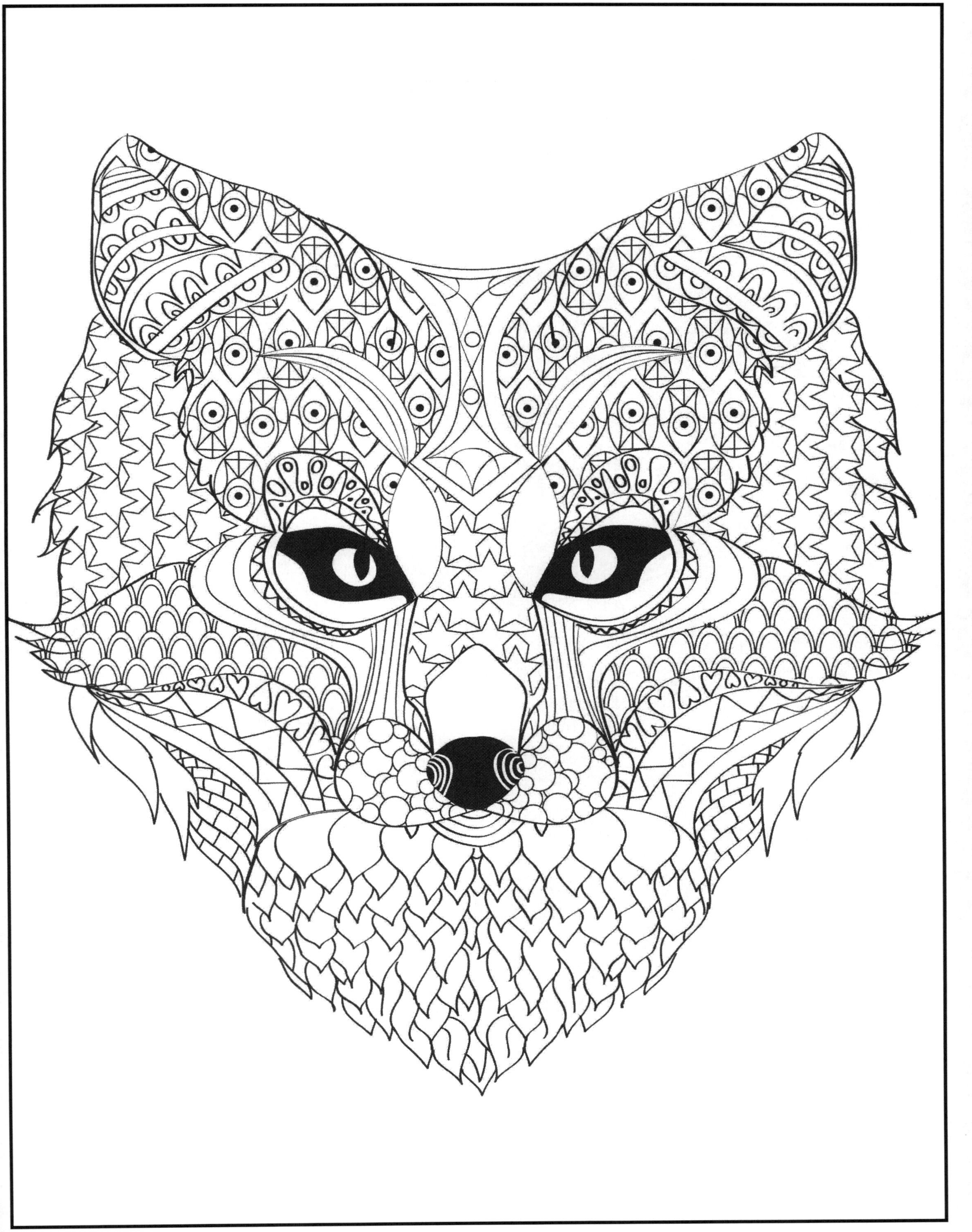

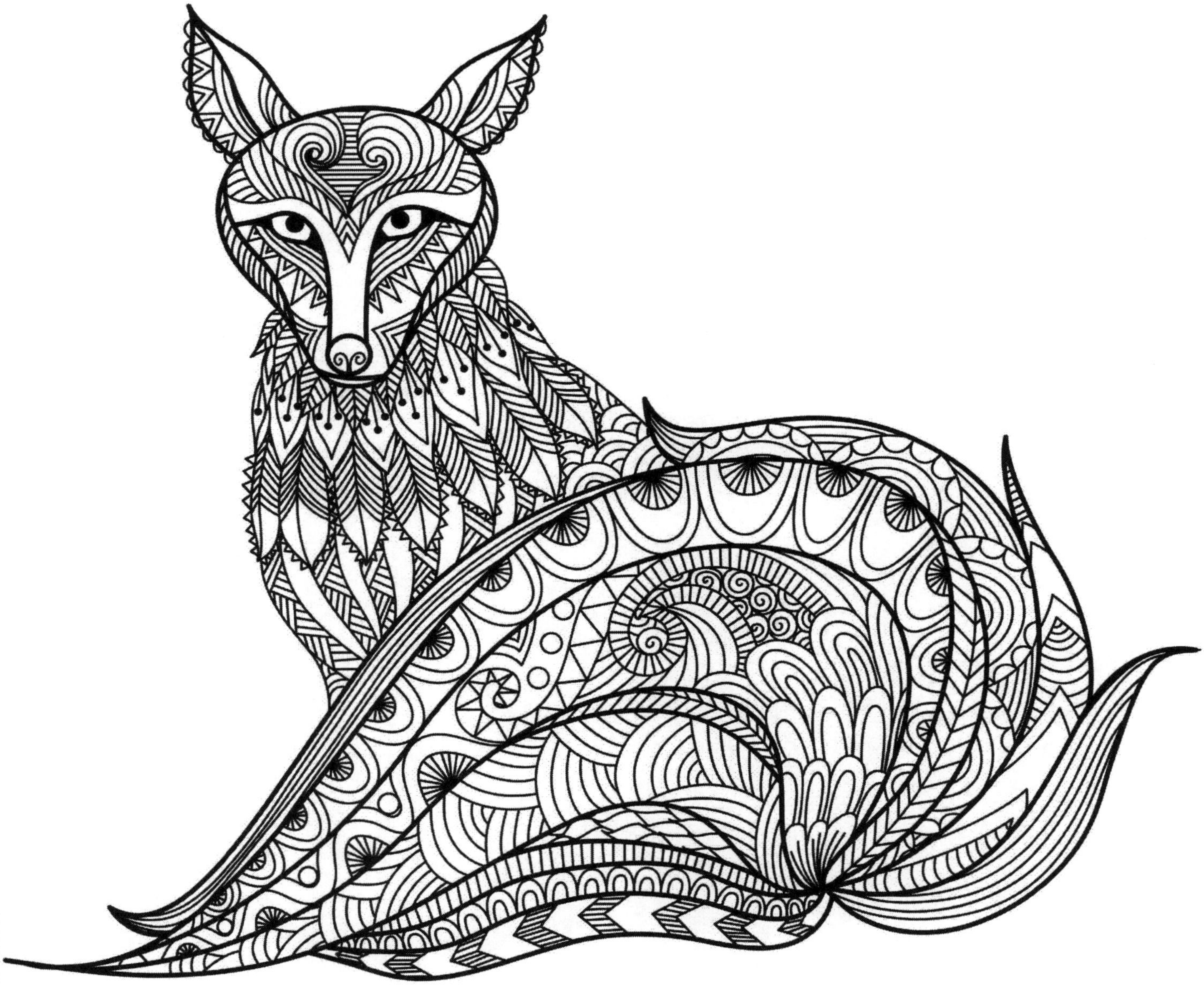

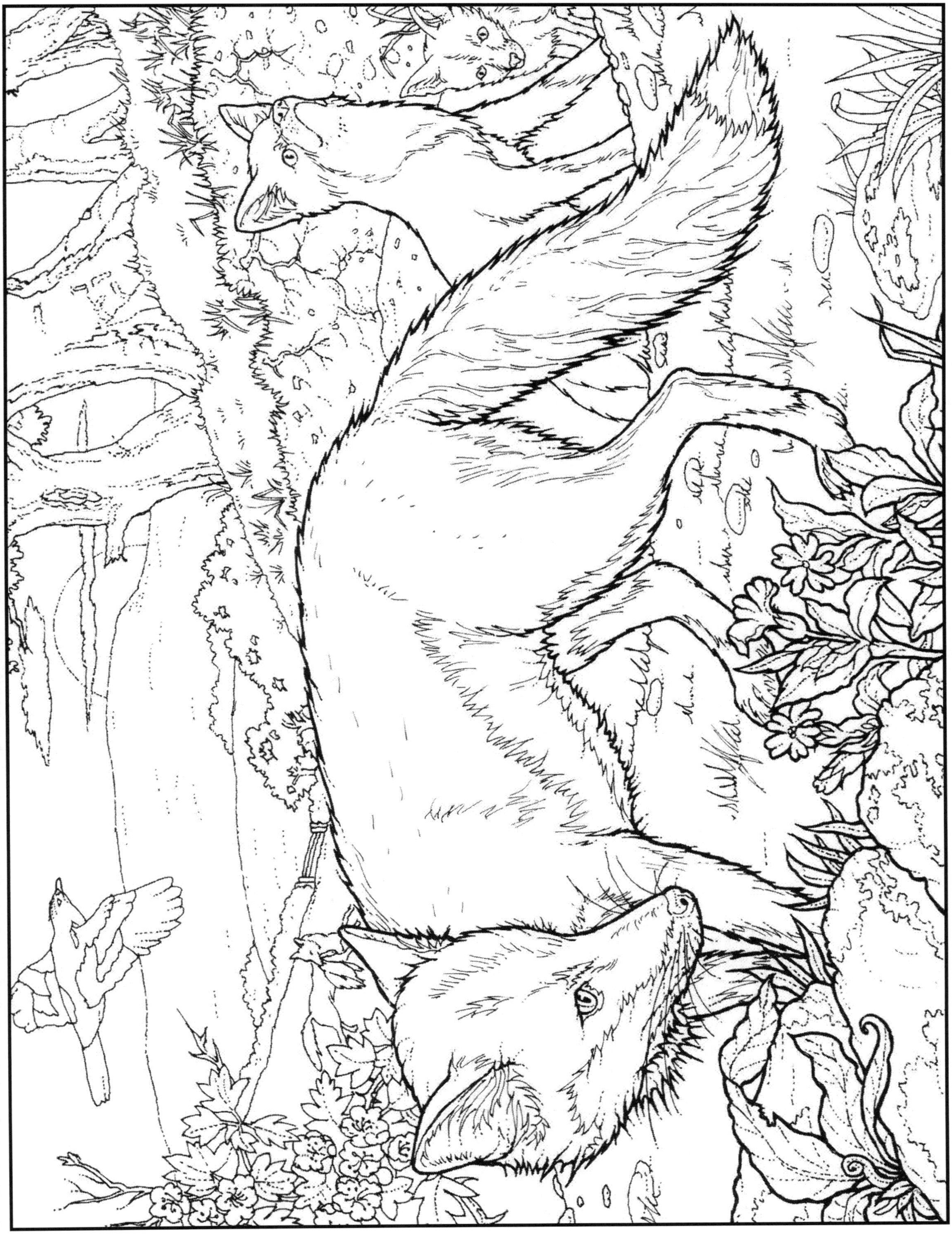

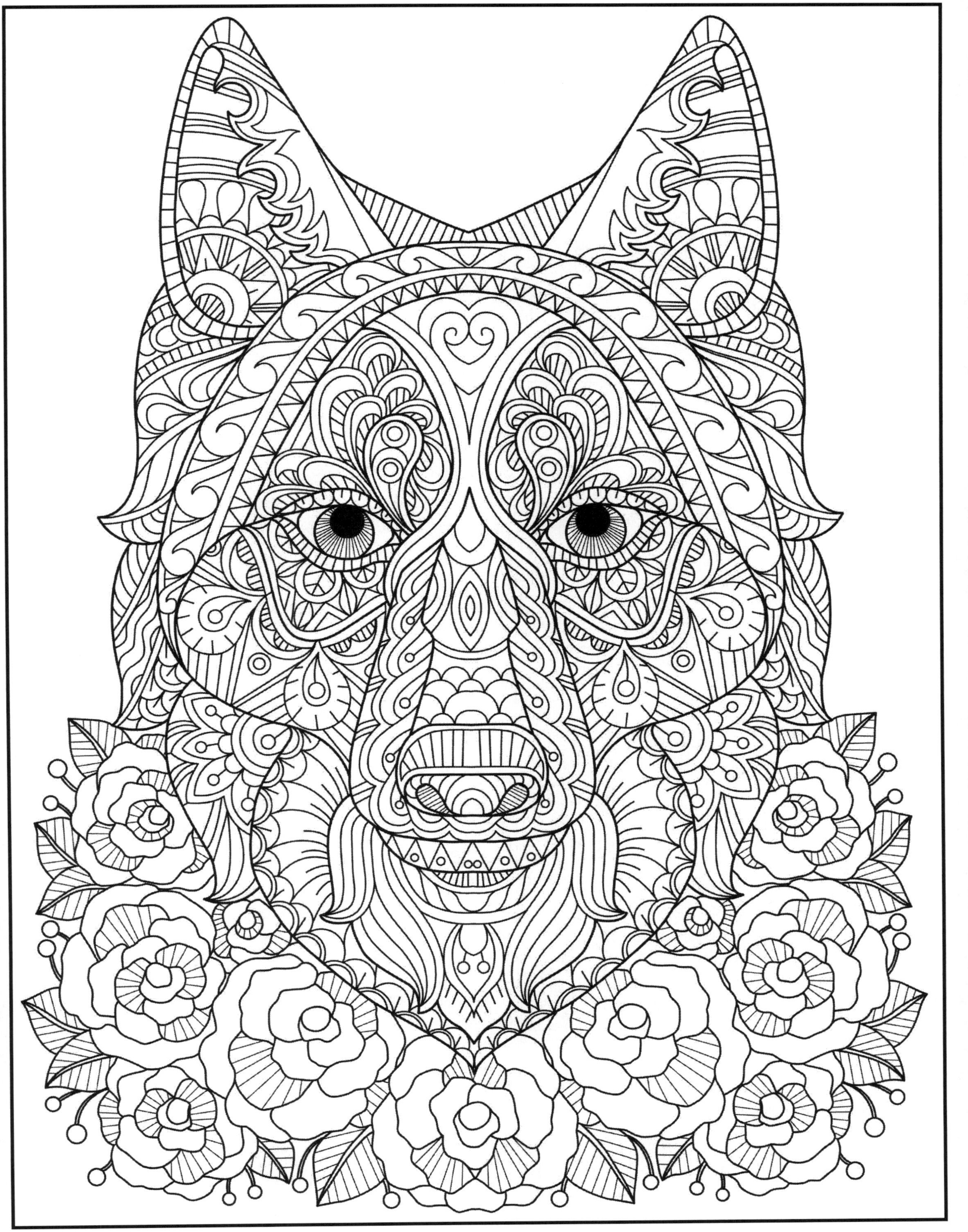

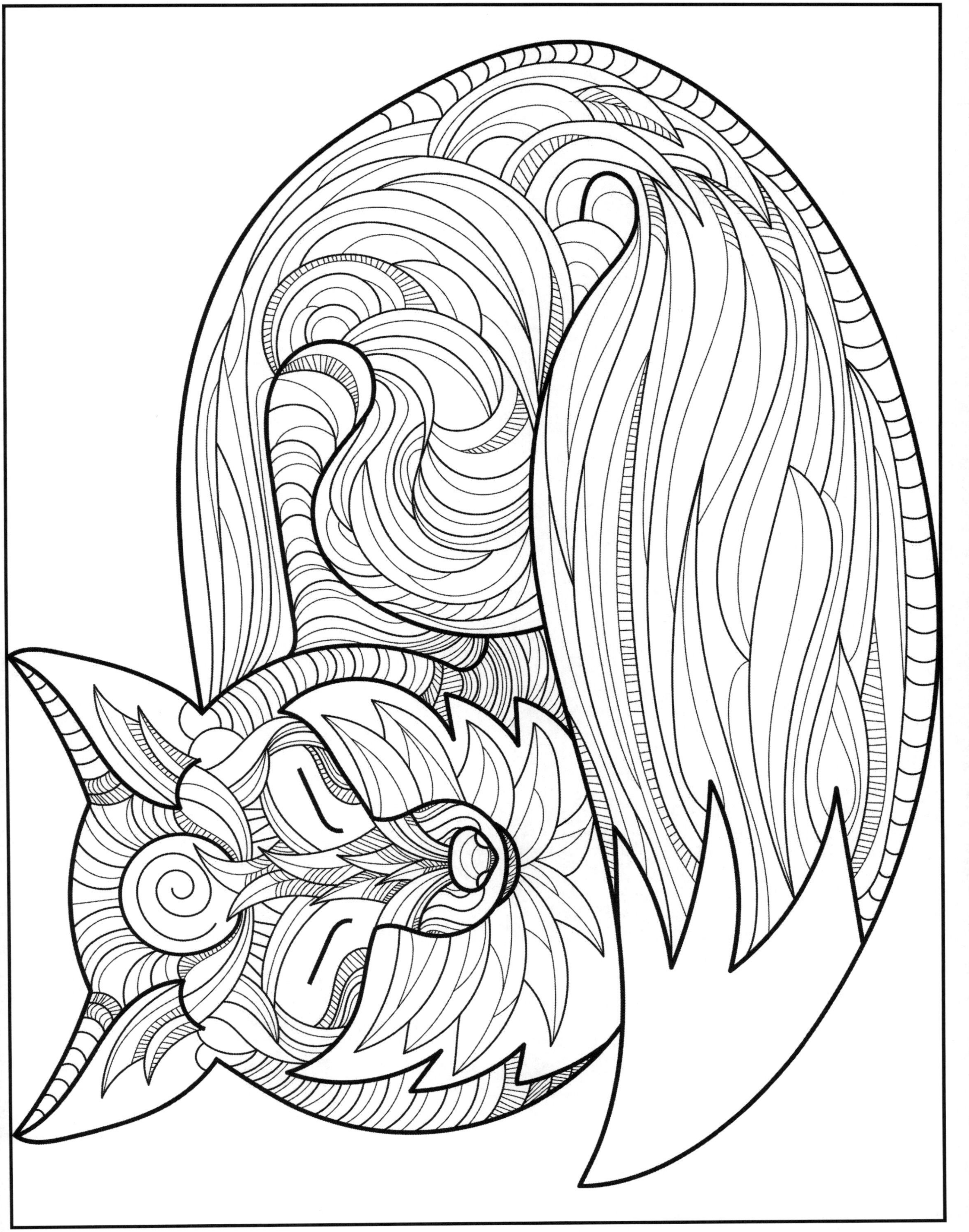

Made in the USA
Middletown, DE
17 February 2023

25077085R00062